The Awesome Game

The Awesome Game

One Man's Incredible, Globe-Crushing Hockey Odyssey

Dave Hill

DOUBLEDAY
CANADA

Doubleday Canada and colophon are registered trademarks of Penguin Random House Canada Limited

Library and Archives Canada Cataloguing in Publication

Title: The awesome game : one man's incredible, globe-crushing hockey odyssey / Dave Hill.
Names: Hill, Dave, 1974- author.
Identifiers: Canadiana (print) 20230207278 | Canadiana (ebook) 20230207286 |
    ISBN 9780385675512 (hardcover) | ISBN 9780385675529 (EPUB)
Subjects: LCSH: Hockey—Anecdotes. | LCSH: Hockey—Social aspects—Anecdotes. |
    LCSH: Hockey players—Anecdotes. | LCSH: Hockey fans—United States—
    Anecdotes. | LCSH: Hill, Dave, 1974-—Travel—Anecdotes. | LCGFT: Anecdotes.
Classification: LCC GV847 .H45 2023 | DDC 796.962—dc23

Drawing on page i and all interior photographs © Dave Hill except: Slava Fetisov, page 64 (photographer: Ian Gava / French Select Collection via Getty Images) and Bryan Trottier, page 239 (photographer: Bruce Bennett / Bruce Bennett Collection via Getty Images)

Printed in the USA

Published in Canada by Doubleday Canada,
a division of Penguin Random House Canada Limited

www.penguinrandomhouse.ca

1st Printing

Penguin
Random House
DOUBLEDAY CANADA

For my dad, Bob Hill Sr.
Sorry about the garage door.

In memory of Barb Kato.
We miss you every day and
watching The Lawrence Welk Show
just isn't the same without you.

CONTENTS

INTRODUCTION

The Sport of the Gods

Ice hockey has always been the sport of the gods to me, a metaphor for life itself where chaos and control, persistence and chance, density and transcendence are all on brash display each and every moment of the game—even between periods, when most people are just using the restroom. And don't get me started on the hair, the discussion of which could fill its own glorious yet deeply disturbing book if my publisher would just cut the damn check already.

The truth is, I've never been much for sports besides hockey. All that screaming, yelling and nacho cheese? Sure, it's fun enough for a little while, but even as a kid, I can remember playing or even just watching sports like baseball, football, basketball, or soccer and eventually thinking, "This needs to stop. Right now."

But with hockey it's always been the exact opposite. I can't get enough of it.

My earliest notions of hockey date back to family trips to the ice skating rink in my youth at the behest of my Canadian grandfather, Clarence Blake Sr.,* the same man who famously and not even slightly rhetorically once posed the question "What good are you if you can't skate?" and, as such, made sure my siblings and I were tossed onto the ice while still in diapers.

It was on one of these outings that I noticed a pair of battered hockey goals stashed in a dark corner of the building just beyond the rink itself. They were mysterious contraptions that, along with the acrid smell of the place, told me there had to be more going on here besides me stumbling around the rink for a few laps before spending the rest of the day spilling hot chocolate down the front of my sweater as I teetered around the concession area on old, hand-me-down skates. Soon, questions were asked, and before long a whole new world was revealed to me, one where grown men with proudly missing teeth barreled down the ice with equal parts abandon and finesse and enough people in the stands thought it was a good idea to occasionally throw a dead octopus onto the ice that it had officially become a "thing."

I followed the usual path of the hockey-obsessed after that, starting with street hockey out in the family driveway, where I broke enough garage windows with the puck that one day my

---

* My grandfather was the primary inspiration for my last book, *Parking the Moose*, a timeless classic about exploring Canada as a result of thinking I was one-quarter Canadian, only to find out . . . well, I don't want to ruin it for you.

dad decided to just board them up altogether rather than go to the trouble of replacing them over and over again. From the driveway, I eventually moved on to playing youth hockey and, on at least one or two occasions, attempting a game of pond hockey by trespassing onto the grounds of a nearby convent, much to the confusion of the nuns—and also me, as I had been talked into it by the big kids.

High school and even a couple years of college hockey followed until the idea of drinking beer and attempting awkward conversation with girls proved preferable to an away game in Poughkeepsie in front of a crowd that consisted of the Zamboni driver and whoever had to lock up at the end of the night.

I had hoped for a long career in the NHL, but, the occasional beer league game aside, it was an early retirement for me. Still, my love for hockey has remained, and along with it, some nagging questions that still go unanswered. For starters, why in the hell don't most Americans love hockey even half as much as I do? I mean, sure, twenty-five out of the thirty-two teams in the NHL are based in the United States, so it's not exactly kiiking* in terms of public visibility. But if you were to ask the average American to choose between watching the Canucks play the Bruins or, say, the latest episode of *Dancing*

---

* Invented in Estonia, kiiking is a sport where people climb up onto a giant swing and attempt to do a full 360-degree revolution, something most of us only dreamed of as kids. Don't feel bad if you've never heard of it—I just found out about kiiking myself, and it's amazing. In fact, seeing to it that kiiking is one day the number two sport in America is next on my to-do list. Or maybe I could just move to Estonia. Whatever it takes.

with the Stars, I bet they'd choose that damn dancing show nine times out of ten.

In America, hockey is known as the proverbial "fourth sport,"* but it's not even that. According to something I just read on the internet, the actual fourth sport is auto racing, specifically NASCAR—which is literally people driving in circles, and nothing else, for hours at a time while people of questionable belief systems watch from the stands, oblivious to the fact that heatstroke is even a thing—with hockey coming in a distant fifth, something that might at least partially explain why, when I ask the bartender to turn on the Rangers game in my neighborhood bar in New York City, he pretends to have lost the remote. Yes, even during the playoffs.

But hockey may not even be fifth. Something else I just read on the internet suggested that the fourth most popular sport in America is actually soccer, which is just a really lazy form of hockey in my expert opinion, even though I'll admit it's fine to watch if there isn't a hockey game on already. So, if NASCAR and soccer are both gunning for fourth place, that would knock

---

* The top three sports in America are, of course, football, baseball and basketball, in that order, at least one of which the rest of the world can barely be bothered with, as best I can tell—something I mention not to suggest that football is stupid, just that it could be argued that the rest of the world seems to think so. And while I'm at it, please know I would also never suggest that hockey is much harder than any of those other sports because you have to learn a whole new mode of transport in the form of ice skating in order to play it instead of just walking or running around like you've been doing your whole life anyway. This is quite simply not an argument you will find in this book that much, however true it may be.

hockey back to sixth place by default, something I can't even consider right now for the sake of my sanity.

Growing up in Cleveland, which hasn't had an NHL team since 1978, things were especially tough for a young hockey fan. In elementary school, a working knowledge of the Browns, Cavs or Indians was valuable social currency, while my enthusiasm for hockey, if anything, only served to further alienate me from my peers.

"Did you see the Flyers game last night?" I might ask a schoolmate at lunch, just looking to make conversation.

"What are the Flyers?" he'd reply before slowly sliding down the bench in search of interaction with literally anyone else. The mere mention of someone like Don Cherry—or even his innocent and not-at-all-controversial dog, Blue—could have me eating alone for weeks.

My own struggles aside, it's not as if there haven't been formal efforts to win more Americans over to the only sport I care about—everything from making the puck look like a damn beach ball on television* so that people might have a better chance of spotting it on the screen to hiring scantily clad women to tidy the ice between plays instead of the usual guy in a windbreaker with

---

* This was done by Fox Sports when it broadcast NHL games between 1996 and 1998. The technology the network used was called FoxTrax, and it involved embedding the puck with shock sensors and infrared emitters so that the puck would glow on TV. And as if all of that weren't enough to blow your mind right out your butt, the guy who came up with this idea was named David Hill, head of Fox Sports at the time. If you're freaking out right now, how do you think I feel?

a shovel. And while ditching the guy in the windbreaker is not entirely without merit, the fact remains that my beloved hockey still has limited appeal in the States, with only a reported five percent of citizens even admitting to liking it, according to another article I just read on the internet. Is this number growing? Sure. But not fast enough for my liking. So there.

Despite its stunted status in America, hockey remains wildly popular in pretty much every other country where the climate requires people to at least occasionally opt for a layered look, from Canada to Germany, Scandinavia, Japan and—you heard me—India. In fact, it is the most popular sport in the world behind soccer and cricket.* I even saw a couple guys carrying hockey equipment to a rink in Nottingham, England, one night a few years ago, something I would have thought was illegal but apparently isn't.

"Hey guys," I asked them. "You going to play some hockey?"

"Yeah," one of them replied before exchanging a concerned look with his buddy and picking up his pace.

I guess they might have thought I was a creep, especially with the way I jumped out from the bushes like that. But I didn't care because I love hockey, and any opportunity to watch or even just talk about it is something I can't bring myself to pass up, even on a cold, damp night in England while otherwise walking alone, just contemplating the night.

While this book will attempt to at least partially answer the question as to why hockey isn't at the top of the heap in terms

---

* Yes, cricket. I know.

of sports in the United States, I'd be lying if I told you it wasn't about a bit of unfinished business, too. You see, like most folks, I've dreamed of doing all sorts of amazing, even gravity-defying things in this lifetime. And while I'm by no means an international superstar in any particular field, if I dare say so myself, I've been fortunate enough to at least nibble a table scrap or two of success in a few of the areas I've set my hand to. But when it comes to hockey, my first love, it's a whole other story. I played for a bunch of years, abruptly stopped one day, and now have pretty much nothing to show for it other than a few scars I would like to think give me a rugged-yet-approachable look, a bag full of moldy old equipment I insist on carting around with me for no good reason every time I move, and a working knowledge of the obscure Canadian hometowns of my hockey heroes that borders on obsessive.

So, on a purely selfish level, this book is also an opportunity for me to reconnect with my first love of hockey as both a fan and player, while attempting to get as close a glimpse of it as possible and, who knows, maybe even rub up on the Stanley Cup or some other cool hockey trophy without getting arrested while I'm at it. One can dream, anyway.

But getting back to you, dear reader, this book is also about celebrating the sport of hockey and, hopefully, along the way, finding its very soul as I connect with people just like you all over the world, people who love this magical game where, yes, at some point in the season, assuming a team is doing well enough, at least one of its fans may go to the trouble of procuring a dead octopus, bringing it with them to the game, and then watching that game with the dead octopus at close reach before eventually throwing the dead octopus out onto the very surface where the game is being played, as if that's a totally reasonable thing for a person to do. And hopefully, while I'm at it, I'll get at least a few people who have no interest whatsoever in the game to understand why I have a closet full of old jerseys in the first place and, who knows, maybe set down the remote next time they stumble upon a game while channel surfing.

And should I succeed in this literary mission, I will take whatever knowledge I have gained and set about helping hockey ascend to its rightful place as at least the fourth most popular sport in the United States.

Take that, NASCAR—you've had it too good for too long.

1

A Scrappy Young Winger from University Heights

I was fourteen years old, and after three mostly uneventful seasons playing youth hockey—unless you count the handful of times I fainted on the ice at early Saturday morning games as a result of having skipped breakfast—it was time to say goodbye to elementary school and move on to the big leagues, which is to say at least try to play for the hockey team at the high school I'd be attending as a freshman the following school year: St. Ignatius, an all-boys Catholic preparatory school located on the mean streets of Cleveland proper.

St. Ignatius was (and still is) a big school, with about 1,500 students from all over the greater Cleveland area. The school mascot is the wildcat, which at the time I mostly just understood to be a cat of indeterminate origin that wasn't exactly crazy about rules. Even so, I was beyond excited at the prospect of becoming a full-fledged St. Ignatius Wildcat, proudly wearing the school's blue and gold colors.

For most sports at the time, St. Ignatius had a varsity, junior varsity and, in some cases, even a freshman team. But for hockey, there was just one: varsity. The prospect of making this team in my freshman year felt like a long shot as, despite no longer sucking, I still lacked the playing experience of all the juniors and seniors already on the team. Also, since I weighed just a hundred pounds and hit puberty roughly fifteen minutes before tryouts, I wasn't what anyone might confuse for menacing, unless you had an irrational fear of acne and poorly conditioned hair. But what I might have lacked in skill or size, I made up for in the one thing I've learned can matter more than anything else in this life when it comes to making things happen: sheer and utter delusion. So, I figured I might still have a shot at making the team if I really gave it my all. Besides, not playing for my high school team would likely mean signing up for another year of youth hockey, which felt like a dead end, given that I was still convinced I had a bright future on the ice despite an abundance of indications to the contrary.

"I'll probably only play a couple seasons of high school hockey against older kids who shave before word of this scrappy young winger from University Heights, Ohio, makes its way to Canada and I'm forced to move north so I can play junior hockey with all the other future Gretzkys," I thought. "I sure hope my family likes Timbits."

For the uninitiated, Timbits are donut holes from Tim Hortons, the popular Canadian donut and coffee concern cofounded by the late hockey great who just so happens to have been named Tim Horton. Timbits come in many flavors—including, I am told, "yeast," which is concerning, but I have no choice but to trust that they know what they are doing. Also, as of this writing, there is a version of Timbits called "Timbiebs," which apparently taste not unlike the Canadian pop star Justin Bieber, depending on whom you ask. In short, I encourage you to try the yeast-flavored Timbits at your earliest convenience.

Anyway, deep down inside, I probably knew I had no real future as a hockey player, but to consciously admit that sort of thing would have meant a loss of innocence, an acknowledgment that maybe all my childhood dreams might not come true after all and I might never play left wing for the Edmonton Oilers or New York Islanders while also—weirdly—being asked to tour with Van Halen during the off-season, even though I'd already promised my *Sports Illustrated* swimsuit model girlfriend we'd just relax at home for the summer. And since I was just fourteen and still largely hairless below the neck, I saw no point in abandoning my dreams just yet.

The tryouts for the St. Ignatius varsity team were pretty grueling, with me trying desperately to keep pace with upperclassmen almost twice my size as we did all the kinds of drills and exercises that were popular in simpler times before parents became litigious. I tried to comfort myself with the fact that Wayne Gretzky himself was smaller and slower than most other guys in the NHL, and since I was the smallest and slowest kid at the varsity tryouts, it only stood to reason I was destined for similar greatness. But it wasn't always enough.

"M-m-must not d-d-die," I remember thinking as I clung to the boards while gasping for breath after every drill. It was only a deep desire to save my dad the embarrassment of having to cart my corpse out of the rink after tryouts that kept me going.

•••

Still, somehow, when it was all over and the coach read aloud the names of all the boys who would be playing for the varsity team that year, I heard mine, along with all the juniors and seniors and just two other freshmen who would be making up the varsity squad that year.

"Looks like you won't need to be driving me over to the Cleveland Heights rink anymore," I told my dad when he got home from work that night. "This kid's playing for the St. Ignatius Wildcats!"

"Congrats!" my dad replied. "What's a wildcat?"

"It's a cat that can't be tamed despite everyone's best efforts, Dad," I told him. "It's right there in the name."*

It's probably worth mentioning at this point that the St. Ignatius hockey team back then was relatively horrible. Sure, there were plenty of good athletes on the team, but it was also a refuge for misfits, delinquents and other types who tended to live

---

* I would like to acknowledge that our conversation may not have gone exactly like that, but I do remember my dad being glad I made the team.

on the fringes of society, at least as far as Catholic boys school went. This being the eighties and all, there were even a couple guys who smoked actual tobacco cigarettes before, after and— I swear at least once, to my memory—during practice. So, while whatever tenacity I might have exhibited during tryouts certainly didn't hurt, the greater likelihood is that I simply didn't suck quite as much as all the other new kids hoping to make the team that year, and that's why I made the cut. Whatever the reason, though, the important thing was that I suddenly became the only one of my friends playing for a varsity sports team.

"That's so cute that you're playing freshman basketball," I'd say dismissively to a classmate. "Must be nice playing with other fourteen-year-olds all the time."

But whatever cool points I thought I might be scoring in homeroom didn't get me far when it came to playing on the team itself, which lacked much of the glamour I figured would be just part of the deal when playing for a varsity team. For starters, practice was at 6 a.m. three days a week before school. Fortunately, a senior on the team named John lived just a few blocks away, so my dad was spared having me to drive me across town at an ungodly hour. Instead, John would pull into my family's driveway at around 5 a.m. on practice days and we'd wend our way through the east-side suburbs of Cleveland, all the way across town to the West Side suburb of Brooklyn, where our home ice was located.

I don't think I'd ever been awake at such an hour, much less been driven through the mean streets of suburban Cleveland in an old Buick, until this point in my life and I was fascinated at the sight of actual people on the street living their lives as we headed to the rink.

"Who are these people?" I wondered. "And where could they possibly be going?"

At the time I assumed they were criminals or some other inhabitants of the ruthless Cleveland underworld, shuffling down the block to go see "the man" or something. But looking back on it, most of them were probably just headed for work on the early shift.

Our soundtrack on the way to practice was WMMS, the local rock station, which played the likes of Ratt, Black Sabbath, Cheap Trick, Led Zeppelin, Quiet Riot and not much else on a constant loop in the early morning hours, which was fine by me, as, at this point in life, I was mostly unaware that there were other forms of music in existence anyway. To this day, whenever I hear Quiet Riot's version of Slade's "Cum on Feel the Noize,"* I am instantly transported back to those early morning drives to practice, the unmistakable funk of stale hockey equipment emanating from the trunk and all.

As it turned out, driving to practice while cranking stone-cold jams was pretty much the highlight of my first year on the high school varsity hockey team, as I mostly sat on the bench, watching

---

* Please note that, while I still very much enjoy Quiet Riot's version of this song, I have since grown partial to Slade's original version, which, if you don't already know it, is a seventies glam rock masterpiece. It's worth noting that Slade's guitar player is also named Dave Hill. And since I probably won't find another opportunity to tell you this in this book, about once or twice a year I receive an email from a confused Slade fan who thinks they are emailing the other Dave Hill, and it thrills me to no end.

our team lose to whoever showed up to play us that day. Sure, we managed to win a game here and there, but we were a motley crew, sort of like the Bad News Bears without the moxie or the Matthau. Our coach at the time even worked as a parole officer by day, which seemed oddly fitting. And, adding to the humiliation of our losing record, we did it while wearing an off-brand version of Cooperalls, the short-lived long hockey pants infamously and very briefly worn by the Philadelphia Flyers and the Hartford Whalers in the early eighties, before the NHL mercifully banned them altogether. I'm guessing the idea of those pants was that they were somehow supposed to make you better at hockey, but they somehow made losing feel even worse.

Also, in an effort to combat the acne mentioned a few paragraphs back, I had started using a product called Oxy Wash that, while not making much of a difference with my skin, did succeed in bleaching the bangs of my Flock of Seagulls–style haircut* bright orange, as I usually neglected to move them away from my face while lathering up. The effect only added to the awkwardness of an already awkward time.

"You dyeing your hair, Hill?" one of my upperclassman teammates would sneer at me like a character from *Lord of the Flies* as I strapped my pads onto my soft, pale flesh before practice.

"No," I'd answer while staring at the rubber matting of the

---

* A Flock of Seagulls, if you don't know, are an English new wave band from Liverpool who were an early staple of MTV, known as much for their long-in-the-front, short-on-the-sides eighties hairstyles as for their catchy, synth-driven pop tunes. Not to be a jerk or anything, but I just looked them up and the lead singer has unfortunately gone bald, while my hair still looks amazing.

locker room floor. I didn't dare explain that my orange hair was actually the by-product of a rigorous skin care regimen, as it might have gotten me killed.

At the start of my sophomore year, we got two new coaches, a couple of guys named Phil and Dave who had actually played college hockey and knew all sorts of things about plays, strategy and other stuff coaches tend to go on about while waving their arms around in front of a dry-erase board. And they made us wear jackets and ties to games to make us look like we had our shit together when we showed up to the rink, even though we still totally didn't.

It was around this time that I finally began to consciously admit to myself that my NHL dreams might slowly be slipping away. In fact, I distinctly remember a pregame warm-up that sophomore season, right around the holidays, and Billy Squier's "Christmas Is the Time to Say 'I Love You'" was blaring from the PA system. And as I skated loops around the rink while intermittently attempting to look cool while stretching my groin, it suddenly occurred to me that I probably had a better shot at becoming the next Billy Squier than I did of becoming the next Wayne Gretzky. And while that definitely didn't happen either, it's fair to say I did come much closer to Squier territory than Gretzky territory in the years that followed.*

---

* In the event you end up taking a break from this gripping tome in the next few minutes, you can see what I mean by going on YouTube and searching for a clip of my first band, Sons of Elvis, performing on Jon Stewart's pre–*Daily Show* program *The Jon Stewart Show* in all our mid-nineties, post-grunge glory.

I never expected Billy Squier to force me to take a good, hard luck in the mirror like that, especially not with a Christmas song that was, with apologies to Billy, one of his lesser works. Still, despite the disturbing realization detailed in the previous paragraph, I decided to give my NHL dreams one last shot by talking my parents into sending me to hockey school at Phillips Exeter Academy in New Hampshire the summer after my sophomore year, a fancy hockey camp that was sort of like some weird combination of *Dead Poets Society* and the Rob Lowe vehicle *Youngblood*. In fact, while I'm probably misremembering this, I think we had to wear matching ties and sport coats under our equipment each day on the ice.

I definitely improved as a result of having attended that fancy hockey school, but looking back, it probably had a greater impact on my parents' finances at the time, as evidenced by the fact that my dad still brings up the cost to this day whenever he has the chance.

"I was just at the grocery store," I might say to him. "Blueberries are so expensive."

"Expensive?" he might reply. "Not as expensive as that hockey school your mother and I sent you to after your sophomore year in high school, I bet. Now *that* was expensive."

Still, it's given me at least a few sentences of fodder for this book, so, Dad, if you're reading this, thank you. I can only assume it feels good to know it wasn't all for nothing.

My junior and senior years playing for the St. Ignatius varsity hockey team were slightly more glamorous. Not only did I get my driver's license and even start to shave every couple weeks whether I needed to or not, but the team itself was finally shaping up to be actually pretty good, thanks in part to the addition of a few younger players who were way better than I was despite my unwillingness to admit it at the time. Suddenly we were winning at least as many games as we were losing, and the teams that used to run up the score on us from the very first period found themselves having to wait until later in the game to do that sort of thing, the very definition of sportsmanship and something we really appreciated.

As an upperclassman, I also finally had the seniority I so desperately craved, so if anyone's hair was getting inadvertently turned orange as a result of his skin care regimen, for example, it would be *my* turn to insult him about it. I don't think I ever did, but it was nice to know I could have if I wanted.

By this point, I had also started writing for the school paper, so when it came time to write an article about the hockey team, I naturally appointed myself for the job as I had yet to learn about stuff like journalistic integrity or what a conflict of interest was, for example. Still, as a reporter, I had a job to do, so I only thought it fair to write about the team as I saw fit. To this day, friends and old teammates remind me how I described myself as having a slap shot that "could destroy a small town." Whatevs.

During my senior year, I even managed to be named an assistant captain of the team, with a big letter *A* added to my jersey and everything. I'm still not entirely sure what the purpose of an assistant captain is, other than to look like the second-coolest guy on the team, but I felt pretty good about it.

On the downside of things, because I wasn't exactly

shattering suburban Cleveland scoring records, the coaches decided to switch me to defense on the off chance that I had been secretly great at that the whole time and had just been keeping it to myself for some reason. As it turned out, I wasn't, but I still saw plenty of ice time, and being on defense allowed me to appreciate the offensive skills of my former forward line-mates from a better vantage point as I watched them operate from just inside the blue line.

Our final game of my senior-year season was against our archrivals, St. Edward High School, another all-boys' Catholic school located on the West Side of suburban Cleveland. St. Ed's, as it was known on the streets, was a powerhouse team coached by Bob Whidden, a former professional goalie who'd played for the WHA's Cleveland Crusaders, something that gave him god status as far as I was concerned. A couple of the guys on the St. Ed's team at the time even ended up going on to play in the NHL. Every time we'd played them previously throughout my illustrious high school career, they had beaten us easily and severely. In fact, it was the very first time I tried to play the puck against St. Ed's forward and future NHLer Todd Harkins during my junior year that I realized just how limited my hockey skills might actually be.

"Oh, so that's how you play hockey," I thought after Todd skated off, having relieved me of the burden of the puck as if I were a small child.

The fact that this happened at Winterhurst, the very same ice rink my mom frequently dragged me to for the public skating sessions with organ accompaniment that my father had somehow talked his way out of, made everything worse. At least then I got a free Coke out of it.

Despite the rivalry between the two schools, one of the things St. Ignatius and St. Ed's had in common was that the girls from the local Catholic girls' high school, Magnificat, tended to date boys from both schools, so on the night of our final matchup of my high school career, the bleachers of our home rink were relatively teeming with teenage girls in addition to all the parents and fellow students in attendance. In short, if there were ever a time to suddenly be amazing at hockey, it was now. And while some of my teammates certainly rose to the occasion, I'm not so sure I did. What I do remember is, despite our best efforts, St. Ed's did what they'd always done when playing hockey against us—beat us mercilessly.

I don't remember the exact score, as I've learned to repress such things, but I do remember being really upset about losing, especially in front of all those girls I was afraid to talk to. And when I got home that night, I was a typical petulant teenager, taking the loss out on my family—especially my parents, as my siblings had the good sense to mostly just ignore me by this point in my life.

What I do remember is my father calmly interrupting me in the middle of my postgame meltdown.

"Dave, you might be upset because high school hockey is over for you and things didn't end exactly how you wanted," he said. "But what you might not realize is that tonight was also the end of high school hockey for me, and I'm not too happy about it, either."

At the time, I chose to find his words just annoying, but at seventeen, I also realized he was also making a profound statement on life, love and family, which, of course, I chose to also find annoying but am happy to report I fully recognize and appreciate as of this writing.

Shortly after my dad said those words to me, I quietly took my blue and gold bag of hockey equipment down to the basement, where it would rot until at the least the following summer. And I didn't give much thought to my high school hockey career in the years that followed, as I'd moved on to attend Fordham University in the Bronx before attempting to navigate young adulthood after that. There's not much time to reflect on high school glories—or a lack thereof—when you've got some credit card collections department breathing down your neck at every turn.

Just a handful of years ago, however, things changed. I was back in Cleveland, performing at a comedy club, and afterward was approached by Pat O'Rourke, the current coach of the St. Ignatius Wildcats varsity hockey team. Pat is a few years younger than I am, so we never skated together, but he played for St. Ignatius back in high school, too. We got to chatting after the show and I was pleased to hear that someone actually remembered that I'd played hockey for the biggest Catholic boys' school in Cleveland at one point in my life, especially after I'd just used so much profanity on stage.

Pat and I kept in touch and he made a point of inviting me to play in the St. Ignatius hockey alumni games that happened every year around the holidays. Somehow the stars never aligned, and I was never in town when the games happened, but the very idea of these games somehow instilled in me some sense of unfinished business, a feeling that maybe I needed a bit of closure on my high school hockey experience.

"You think there's any chance I might come skate with you and the team at practice one of these days?" I decided to ask Pat over email one day.

"Sure," he replied. "You know, if you really want to."

It was all the encouragement I needed. So, on my next visit back to Cleveland, I was sure to dig my bag of old hockey equipment out of the back of the closet and bring it along for the trip, no matter how much it annoyed my girlfriend and dog on the drive.

A couple days later, back in Cleveland, I loaded my equipment into the car and pointed it in the direction of Brooklyn Recreation Center, the very same rink where we used to play when I was in high school. On the drive over, it occurred to me that it was my first time coming anywhere even near the rink since that last game we lost against St. Ed's, probably in the interest of self-preservation. And as I pulled into the parking lot, I was pleased to find it looked exactly the same all these years later. I even remembered the exact parking spot John used to pull his Buick into at the side of the building so we could crank tunes while we waited for the other guys to arrive for practice in the morning.

I grabbed my equipment from the trunk and headed for the entrance, where I immediately ran into a young woman sitting behind the ticket window.

"I-I'm here for the St. Ignatius hockey practice," I stammered, assuming she needed some concrete explanation as to why a middle-aged man was standing there with a hockey stick and bag of equipment on a Tuesday afternoon.

"Yeah, just head in," she said, seemingly not nearly as concerned about things as I was.

As I headed toward the locker rooms, I spotted a big door with the St. Ignatius logo on it, which was impressive since, back when I played, the team didn't have its own designated locker room—we just made use of the same ones everyone else used, from eight-year-old mite players straight on up to drunken men's leaguers.

"I'm here to skate with St. Ignatius," I said to a twentysomething guy standing in the hallway who I figured must work there, given his official-looking windbreaker.

"Sure thing," he said, heading toward me with a softball-sized ring of keys in his hand.

He opened the door to reveal an NHL-worthy locker room, complete with those individual stalls for each player that you always see the pros standing in front of while emotionlessly talking about "shots on goal" and "getting pucks in deep" during all those hockey interviews on TV. The walls above the stalls were covered with various St. Ignatius team jerseys from throughout the years, including the one my team used to wear back in the eighties. Also on display were something completely unfamiliar to me back when I played: big, shiny trophies the team had been awarded after winning multiple state championships. You see, somewhere along the way, and largely thanks to Coach Pat, the St. Ignatius Wildcats varsity hockey team had actually gotten *good*. Great, in fact.

"Eric says the hockey players are like the rock stars of the school now," my buddy Tim, whose son had just graduated from Ignatius the year before, told me.

Even though I had absolutely nothing to do with it, I felt a sense of great pride. Back when I was in high school, football was the big sport and the hockey team was just above golf, bowling and something called the "circus club"* in terms of respectability in the school hallways and cafeteria. Also, in addition to the varsity team, the school now has four other hockey teams for junior varsity and freshman players representing the school.

With practice scheduled to start in just a few minutes, I was still somehow the first one in the locker room. I decided to take advantage of this by putting on all of my equipment as quickly as possible, as I figured this might somehow make things less weird, though I'm not sure how or why. If anything, it probably just made things weirder, as though I'd maybe even been sleeping in the locker room overnight in full equipment, just waiting for the team to arrive, like someone destined for some sort of watch list.

As I opened my equipment bag, it dawned on me that I hadn't donned any of this stuff since the last time I played men's-league hockey in Central Park at least fifteen years prior. And even then, most of my equipment had been left over from high school and the season and a half I'd played back in college, which would literally make all of my equipment older

---

* My memory on this is fuzzy, but, as I recall, the circus club mostly trafficked in juggling, the occasional unicycle, and scampering about as if being chased by a bear.

than any of the current players on the St. Ignatius team by at least ten years.

I quickly threw on my pads and covered them with some bright red sweatpants I'd borrowed from my girlfriend Kathy's nephew and a jersey—in this case, a Barrie Colts jersey I'd brought just for the occasion—so as to avoid too much embarrassment once the players and coaches started to arrive. But as I stood there all alone in my vintage hockey equipment in the locker room, I realized I still must have looked like one of the players from an imaginary hockey-based version of the Kevin Costner vehicle *Field of Dreams*. I decided to distract myself from this fact by grabbing a nearby roll of tape and carefully applying it to my old wooden stick, which had been worn down after being pulled into use for street hockey some years back.

After a few more minutes, the coaches and players began to arrive, including the one person I actually knew, Coach Pat.

"Those should be in a museum," Pat said, noting my weathered blue Koho hockey gloves.

"They protect your entire forearm," an assistant coach named Rob laughed.

"Yeah, my dad bought these for me right before sophomore year," I told him, thinking back to the days when these ancient hand shields were state-of-the-art.

Most of the players seemed not to notice me as they filed into the locker room and settled into stalls on the opposite locker room despite my desperate attempts to make eye contact and nod knowingly as if to say, "Don't mind me—I'm just a fellow St. Ignatius Wildcat hockey player looking to completely destroy you once we hit the ice." The few who did notice me appeared to be giggling, though I'd like to think they were just remembering a joke they had heard earlier or something. Regardless, as I stared them down, I noticed that they were all roughly the same size and even had the same haircut, a mid-length wavy hairstyle that was, to be fair, not unlike my own, only without the gray. Back when I played on the team, we looked more like the bar scene in *Star Wars*, with players of all shapes and sizes, some of whom barely appeared to share even basic human genetics.

"This team seems pretty different from back when I was on the team," I said, stating the obvious to Pat as he laced up his skates.

"Yeah," he replied. "It is."

Then we just sat there, nodding momentarily like two people trying to avoid talking about what happened back in the war.

"We're running late today because there was a winter sports rally," Pat then said, breaking the silence.

I was both surprised and disappointed to hear this. I was surprised because, as I remember it, football was the only sport there seemed to be any collective enthusiasm for when I went to St. Ignatius. And I was disappointed, as it's been a long-held dream of mine to one day go back and speak at my alma mater, and I think I would have really hit it out of the park at a winter sports rally despite the fact that I just used a baseball metaphor to drive that point home—and *that* sport is usually played in fall at the high school level.

Moments later, I walked down the familiar hallway toward the rink, stepped out onto the Brooklyn ice rink for the first time in over thirty years and quickly set about doing every pregame stretch I could remember in the interest of fitting in with the other players.

"Last thing I need is another pulled groin, y'know what I'm sayin'?" I tried to say to one of the players in hopes of bonding as he skated by. I don't think he heard me, though.

Once I finished doing all the stretches I could think of, I grabbed one of the many stray pucks on the ice and began firing it against the boards and into the empty nets at each end of the rink as hard as I could without falling down. And as I did so, I couldn't help but briefly fantasize that I was taking part in an NHL pregame warm-up, just as I had done literally every time I hit the ice before a hockey practice or game in my entire life. A little sad, perhaps, but what are we without our dreams?

Anyway, after a couple minutes of that, Pat called all the players to center ice to go over a few bits of hockey business before introducing me to the team.

"Joining us today is Dave Hill," Pat told the players. "He played for Ignatius back in the eighties."

I'm pretty sure I heard an audible gasp from a few of the players as they realized a geriatric would be skating with them today, but I tried not to let it get to me.

"Dave is one of the more well-known graduates of the school," Pat continued, "though not for hockey."

That "not for hockey" part stung momentarily, but I had no choice but to admit that this was my own hang-up as most people on earth probably have no idea I ever played hockey unless they are reading this book.

The formalities out of the way, we split up into two teams of two lines each, with me playing on the second line with Coach Pat. And while I normally would have sat on the team bench until it was my turn to hit the ice, all the players on the team just hopped up onto the boards while they waited, so, after a few unsuccessful tries at lifting my elderly frame up, I did the same in the interest of blending in. In fact, I'd like to think that for someone watching practice from the very top row of the bleachers on the other side of the rink without their glasses, it was next to impossible to tell I wasn't a regular member of the team.

Until I hit the ice, that is, at which point there might have been hints that I was several decades older than all the players on the team and hadn't played hockey, even in a pickup game, since the mid-2000s. This is when the fact that I was technically playing on the second line as a sixth skater—an elusive third defenseman, in fact—really came in handy as I could just kind of hover in the general vicinity of the action and still feel like I was a part of things without having any real responsibility out there on the ice. And since I had read that Gordie Howe used to intentionally cheap-shot his opponents when the refs weren't looking so they would know better than to come near him on the ice, in the event that I inadvertently found myself playing the puck against a member of the opposite scrimmage team, I made a point of engaging in some light, mostly symbolic cross-checking and slashing. This way, if these kids didn't already think I was slightly unhinged for showing up today, my actions would remove all doubt.

Thanks to the fairly regular running and biking I get up to while no one is watching, I'm proud to say I wasn't entirely ready to keel over after each shift. Still, as I watched the clock in between shifts, I had to admit this was easily the longest hour and fifteen minutes of my entire life.

With just a few minutes to go, I hit the ice for what would prove to be my last shift of the scrimmage. And I have no idea if Pat maybe said something to his players to allow the following scenario to happen, but at one point I found myself blazing (relatively speaking, of course) down the left side of the rink on a breakaway. It was at this point that I could have sworn I heard the screams of all those teenage girls who used to come watch us play back in high school, even though—let me be clear—they are all middle-aged women now. Then, as a couple players from the opposing side began to bear down on me, I drew my ancient wooden stick back at the top of the circle and fired one of my trademarked small-town-destroying slap shots at the net, sending it toward the top left corner, stick side—what's known as the "three hole" to us hockey player types. It's at this point that I'd like to tell you how the goalie, this damn child standing in front of the net that afternoon, never saw it coming, that the puck hit the back of the net and my temporary linemates all tackled me in celebration immediately afterward. But as it turned out, the little bastard batted the puck away as if it were a balloon at a child's birthday party, after which I went and grabbed the boards behind the goal line and tried to force oxygen back into my lungs as quickly as possible.

"Too bad you didn't get that one," Pat told me as I finally caught up with the play in the other direction. "That would have been a great finish to practice."

"Yep," I nodded from behind my old wire face mask.

As the years wear on, I could probably adjust my memories so that I did, in fact, end up scoring at the end of practice that day. I'll just have to make a mental note never to read this chapter once I've finally turned this book in.

"You skate the same way you did back in high school," Pat told me as we headed for the locker room after practice. "A lot of people lose it over time, but you've still got it."

I decided it was best not to ask Pat to clarify exactly what "it" was and just be glad I made it to the end of practice in one piece. I did, however, think to ask Pat if, you know, hypothetically speaking, I were a teenager again, I would be good enough to make the current varsity team. But before I had a chance, Pat surprised me by giving me his hockey gloves, an official St. Ignatius hockey pair with "Wildcats" on them and everything.

"Don't worry," Pat told me. "I have another pair at home I can use."

I took this as a sign that, at the very least, I could probably join the team for practice next time I'm in town. And if I'm wrong, guys, let this be your warning to advise the young woman at the ticket window out front not to let me in so easily next time.

As it turned out, the St. Ignatius team had a game in town the next day against the Gilmour Academy Lancers. Growing up, my friends and I thought of Gilmour as a fancy school that was far too soft for us street toughs living a couple suburbs away. And while I now realize we were lacking in self-aware-ness to think like that back then, the fact that Gilmour Academy has its own hockey rink on campus also makes me think we were at least partially right. Regardless, you can bet I bor-rowed my girlfriend's mom's car again so I could witness the matchup in person.

Once inside the fancy rink, I was thrilled to be able to grab a front-row seat for myself at center ice. As high school sport-ing events tend to be social affairs, I'll admit to feeling a little bit self-conscious since, as best I could tell, I was the only person in attendance watching the game all by himself. Still, I felt it was my duty to root for my alma mater as best I could, occasionally giving the thumbs-up to Coach Pat and the team on their bench on the other side of the ice, even though they probably didn't see me. I was also sure to glare at any and all Gilmour students as they passed by me on their way to their seats with a look in my eye that I'd like to think said something along the lines of "Your youth will fade and your bodies will one day betray you. Also, Ignatius is going to destroy Gilmour today. Oh, and the fact that I am literally the only person here today sitting all alone isn't weird, so don't even think that for a second."

Adding to my excitement, someone brought a Newfoundland dog to the game, so, since that particular breed is among my very favorite living things, I didn't hesitate to pet it each and every time it happened to pass in front of me.

In short, I was having a pretty amazing time as soon as I sat down. Still, I had a game to focus on. And as I sat there in the front row, I realized it was the closest I'd been to a live hockey game since I'd stopped playing myself, and it didn't take long to get caught up in the excitement as soon as the puck dropped in the opening face-off. Next thing I knew, I was banging on the glass and yelling at the players like Dennis Hopper in *Hoosiers* in that one scene where he shows up to the game hammered and Gene Hackman has to cart his ass out of there. And yes, I realize that is at least the fourth film reference I have made in this chapter. Stop counting.

Despite my enthusiasm, the Ignatius team had a fairly rough go of it early on, tying with Gilmour 1–1 at the end of the first period after having spent much of it in their own defensive zone. As the team headed for their locker room after the buzzer, it occurred to me that maybe this was the perfect opportunity to deliver that rousing speech I'd been fantasizing about all these years. But then along came that Newfoundland again, and I got distracted and forgot about it.

But were it not for that adorable dog happening by again, I probably would have headed over to the Ignatius locker room to deliver that speech, whether they wanted me to or not. I'd like to think it would have gone a little something like this:

"You guys disgust me!* Also—real quick—it just now

---

* As this is the opening line of my speech, I'd make a point of saying it just as I was slamming a locker door, kicking over a trash can, and/or soiling myself for emphasis, all proven attention-getting techniques when delivering an important locker room and/or motivational speech. Also, guys, if you're reading this, you don't disgust me and never have, not in the least. It's just that belittlement is a key ingredient to inspiring others to do better.

occurred to me that some of you maybe didn't see me with my helmet off yesterday and, as a result, have absolutely no idea who I am. So, before I continue, I just wanted to be clear that I'm Dave, the slightly older guy who skated with you guys at practice yesterday, even though a lot of you guys probably assumed I was some amazing transfer student who just got off the plane from Sweden or something because I'm so good at hockey and about five hundred other things I don't even have time to get into right now.

"Anyway, where was I? Oh yeah, you guys disgust me! And you can bet your ass I didn't insist on borrowing my girlfriend's mom's car, even though she said she needed to use it to go to Joann Fabrics today, just so I could come watch you guys sit around in your own defensive zone like you're having a damn picnic with little sandwiches and soda pops and potato chips and whatever else people have at picnics!*

"Do I need to remind you guys that you're playing against a team that calls themselves the Lancers, fer Chrissakes?! Last I checked, a lancer is just a guy with a stick! Let me ask you this: You think a guy with stick has a chance against a wildcat, some rule-hating cat from parts unknown that we'll

---

* I'm guessing it's right around this point that Coach Pat or one of the assistant coaches would probably try to quietly pull me aside and ask me to return to the stands, but that's when I'd just hold my hand up while staring at the floor as if to say, "Dammit, just let me have this one! Besides—we could have avoided this whole scenario if I'd just been invited to the winter sports rally! How hard could it have been?!"

never understand in a million trillion years?!* Hell no! Not on my watch!

"Now, before I walk out of here to grab something at the concession stand before they close for the day, at least according to a sign they had hanging up over the trash can, I have just one question for you: Are you guys gonna go out there and keep acting like you're having a damn picnic out there, or are you gonna maim these pathetic '*Lancers*' like only a Wildcat can? Are you gonna just sit there while they skate rings around you, or are you gonna put the puck in their frickin' net?! Are you gonna get us a *W*, or are you gonna make me wish I'd just let my girl-friend's mom use her car to go to Joann Fabrics today after all, even though I'm pretty sure that place is open until nine and she can just go whenever I get back with the car? The choice is yours, boys. The choice. Is. Yours! Also, yes, I realize I just asked you three questions instead of one. I'm not an idiot!"

Then I'd probably walk out of the locker room and go grab something from the concession stand before the next period

---

* Please note that I just finally got around to googling what exactly a wildcat is, and as it turns out, it's a very specific species of cat, and not just some ran-dom cat with a penchant for mischief as I had previously and repeatedly sug-gested. I apologize for my ignorance on this subject. It's just that we didn't have the internet back when I was in high school. Also, our logo at the time was very stylized, so I could only assume that the wildcat was, in fact, a totally made-up cat and not a totally real cat that, it turns out, you can find in Europe, Africa and even Asia if you play your cards right (or wrong, depend-ing on how you look at it). Also, a lancer carries a lance, which is more like a massive spear, but I wouldn't have had the heart to tell the guys that, as I feel it would have lessened the impact of my speech.

started, just like I'd mentioned during the speech. I don't know why they always close the concession stand early at sporting events. It's not like people stop being hungry or thirsty toward the end of the game. In fact, it's usually just the opposite. Wake up, concession industry!

As it turned out, though, my speech was totally unnecessary as the St. Ignatius team went out there, took back control of the game and beat Gilmour, 3–2.

Sometimes it's the speeches you *don't* give that make all the difference.

2

Katowice Nights

I was in the early stages of plotting and planning for the very book you hold in your hands right now when my brother Bob casually mentioned to me that his wife and my sister-in-law Janyce's cousin's son—which is to say Janyce's first cousin once removed, for all you genealogy buffs—Al Rogers was playing professional hockey in Poland.

"How am I just now hearing this?" I asked Bob, mildly enraged, as if I'd known I had a distant relative who was amazing at hockey, I obviously could have been vicariously enjoying his hockey career for years by now while going to a bunch of games and demanding some kind of recognition as I sat and made a spectacle of myself in the stands, no doubt shirtless and hastily painted from the waist up in the colors of whatever team Al happened to be playing for at the moment. Now that I think about it, I suppose that's exactly why my brother and his wife never mentioned Al's hockey career to me before. But that's something I can address at a future family get-together, preferably while at least slightly overserved.

What matters, though, is that my sister-in-law Janyce's first cousin once removed Al Rogers was playing goal for not one but two professional hockey teams in Poland: GKS Katowice of the Polish Hockey League, the country's premier league, and KS Katowice Naprzód Janów, which used to be a part of the Polish Hockey League but, due to some money issues, now play in the Polish 1. Liga, the second-highest level of hockey in Poland.

In keeping with modern times, I decided to stalk Al on Instagram, and after a bit of back and forth, we eventually hatched a plan for me to wing it on over to Poland so I could catch a few games and hopefully talk about Polish hockey and stuff while having a really nice time in Poland.

I had been to Poland once before, in 2019 to be exact, to perform a comedy show in the beautiful city of Kraków, where I spent a delightful pierogi-, vodka- and mirth-filled thirty-six hours before hopping a bus south through Slovakia to Budapest for more of the same. But this time I would be, of course, headed to Katowice, a former coal mining town and the eleventh-largest city in Poland, with a population of just under 300,000. I'm guessing it's not a big tourist destination for most Americans, especially not in the dead of winter. But as for me, I couldn't wait to Katowice it up. Also, real quick—in case you're wondering, Katowice is pronounced "Kat-o-VEETZ-ah," and not "KAT-o-wiss" as I had been originally convinced. A mnemonic device I've found helpful in remembering this is "Katowice rhymes with pizza. Sort of."

To get to Katowice, I took an overnight flight from JFK to Warsaw before hopping a tiny prop plane, the kind that looks like the pilot might also load the luggage and take drink orders, to finally arrive at the Katowice airport the following evening. From there, I impressed myself—and, I'd like to think, everyone else at the airport—by successfully boarding a bus supposedly headed for downtown Katowice. But as I tried to follow the route on my phone shortly after boarding, I quickly realized the bus was going another way entirely.

"We could be going anywhere right now!" I thought, equally nervous and excited. "This must be how dogs feel whenever they get in a car."

For a solid ten minutes, it seemed like I might be headed for neighboring Belarus or Lithuania, maybe even to start a new life for myself, but in the end, the bus stopped a few blocks from my hotel, just as I'd originally been led to believe it would. I nodded at the three sixtysomething, presumably Polish guys who rode the bus with me and got off, delighted to finally be setting foot in Katowice proper, land of the Polish hockey gods—at least as far as I was concerned, anyway.

A few minutes later I arrived at Hotel Katowice, chosen because it was the first place that came up after I plugged the words "hotel" and "Katowice" into a Google search. A little on the nose, maybe, but I figured with a name like that, it couldn't possibly be located on the outskirts of town, and I was delighted to find I was absolutely right. In fact, it turned out Hotel Katowice is located just down the street from the Spodek Arena, where the GKS Katowice hockey team plays, so I was really nailing it as far as convenience was concerned. Even better, the Hotel Katowice looks like it hasn't been renovated in the least since about 1965, complete with rotary telephones in the hallway on each floor, should you need to call someone from the past, and blood-red carpet that seemed perfect for hiding actual blood. Since I enjoy a hotel with a bit of character just so long as that character doesn't also involve my own murder, I was positively thrilled.

I had hoped to meet up with Al as soon as I rolled into town, but he had practice that evening with the Naprzód Janów team. So, after dropping my bags in my room and splashing a bit of water on my face in hopes that it might help me adjust to the six-hour time difference, I decided to hit the town in search of some dinner and a bottle of anything.

I made it about two blocks from the hotel when suddenly a police car with lights flashing and siren blaring screeched up to the curb next to me, practically taking me out at the knees. I assumed there must have been some caper or another happening right next to or directly behind me that I was somehow oblivious to, but after a quick look around, I realized the person of interest in this particular case was me, Dave, man of action.

The Polish language can sound a little harsh, sometimes even in the politest of conversation, at least to my Midwestern ears, but when a Polish policeman starts yelling at you from his car five minutes after you roll into town, it sounds downright mean. I have no idea what this cop was saying, but he waved his arms to suggest that I should go stand alongside the nearest building immediately, so I did just that. Then the Polish policeman jumped out of his car to yell at me some more while his partner stayed inside the car to glare at me in judgment from the relative comfort of the passenger seat.

"Gentleman, you must have me mistaken for the king of the Polish underworld," I thought to say. "Perfectly understandable."

But instead I just began saying, "English! English!" over and over again in a pitch just slightly higher than my normal speaking voice.

"You see how cross street?!" the policeman then yelled, accommodating my language request.

"I no know," I replied, unconsciously matching his broken English with broken English, something I always seem to do in such situations as a result of some rare psychological condition I am confident exists.

Then the policeman began yelling at me some more. As it turned out, I had crossed the street against the crosswalk signal, a big no-no in Poland, it would seem.

"I'm sorry," I said, straightening up a bit. "I'm visiting from New York City and didn't know."

"You no have crossing signals in New York City?" the other policeman suddenly chimed in from inside the car.

I wanted to tell the Polish policeman how, yes, indeed we do have crossing signals in New York City, but we New Yorkers are lawless types who tend to just cross the street when it seems like a good idea rather than in accordance with what the crossing signal might be instructing us to do at that given moment. But I figured that would only enrage him further, so instead I employed a tactic I've found usually works like a charm in these situations—explain to them that I am a complete idiot.

"I get confused very easily," I told the two officers. "The lights, the sounds, the big buildings—I don't understand any of it. In fact, back home I don't normally even walk around alone. But tonight I had no choice, as I came here all by myself on a big airplane that had snacks."

I figured if I just insulted myself it would take some of the fun out of it for them and they might lose interest in berating me further. I could tell my plan was working, too, as the Polish policemen then just looked at each other for a moment before the one that started in on me in the first place suddenly said, "Be careful—you don't want get hit by car."

"No, I not," I replied. "I do better—I promise."

"And there is big fine if you crossing wrong again!" he added.

It occurred to me at this point that I should maybe mention that I was friends with the goalie for not just one but both of the local pro hockey teams, as I figured that might score some points with these police officers, thus allowing me to cross the street at will for the remainder of my visit to their fair city. But since I had technically not even met Al yet, I saw no sense in dragging him into my life of crime. Instead, I just apologized again and continued on my way as the Polish police officers drove off, presumably in search of other folks easily given to mischief.

Slightly rattled by my Polish police encounter, I walked another couple blocks while being careful to obey any and all pedestrian rules and regulations before I stumbled upon a bar located right next to a sketchy-looking underpass I'm guessing my new police buddies were more than familiar with, as it looked like the perfect spot for just about any criminal behavior one could think of. I decided to head inside to get my bearings and a beer.

"Hi," I said to a young female bartender as I settled into a seat at the bar.

She replied with a combination of Polish and English words to let me know her English wasn't much better than my Polish. It's at this point that I remembered my brother had told me to download a translation app for just such occasions, and I decided to give it a whirl.

"Beer, please," I said into my phone.

"*Poprosze piwo*," the voice of a guy who sounded like he had his shit together way more than I did emanated from my phone seconds later.

Between that and a little bit of pointing at the bottles on the back wall of the bar, I managed to order a dark Polish beer I can't remember the name of but that did the trick just fine.

"I live in New York City," I told the bartender with some more help from my phone in the interest of making small talk as we were the only two people in the place. "I'm here to watch hockey games. Professional hockey games. Here in town, where there are two pro hockey teams."*

---

* Here is how you say it in Polish like the guy on my phone, in case you want to practice: "*Jestem tutaj, aby oglądać mecze hokejowe. Profesjonalne gry w hokeja. Tu w mieście, gdzie są dwie profesjonalne drużyny hokejowe.*"

She smiled and nodded as if to suggest she couldn't wait to hear what my phone and I might say next, so I decided to tell her how I was friends with Al Rogers, the goalie for not one but both of the aforementioned pro hockey teams, in hopes that it would lead to me never having to pay for another beer in this bar again even though, yes, I still hadn't even met Al yet.

She smiled and nodded at that, too, before typing into her own app to inform me that she wasn't a hockey fan, at which point I considered storming out of the place before just acting like I didn't hear her and ordering some fries instead.

After a few more minutes of awkward phone-enabled conversation between me and the bartender, a thirtysomething guy who seemed to know the bartender walked in, bellied up to the bar and immediately started talking to me in Polish, something I took as a compliment, as I assumed it must have meant that I was doing a great job of fitting in.

"English," I said to him with an apologetic shrug.

When he didn't say anything after that, I decided to make use of my phone again and tell him that thing about how I was friends with Al Rogers, the goalie for not one but both of the local pro hockey teams, only I upgraded things a bit this time by telling the guy that Al was actually my best friend in the whole world and we totally hang out all the time—just to see where that might get me in terms of cool points at this particular bar on a cold Thursday night in Katowice, Poland, even though, yes, I know, Al and I had still yet to actually meet.

He raised his eyebrows and nodded in a manner I'd like to think suggested he was impressed before turning back to the bartender and saying a few things in Polish that I wasn't quick enough with my phone to translate for myself. I can only assume he was just telling her he thought I was a really cool guy with cool friends or something like that.

Confident in the knowledge that I'd made a lasting impression on the bartender and the one other guy sitting at the bar, I headed off into the night in search of some proper dinner. But since I'd only mastered asking for beer and fries at this point in my journey, I just stopped off at another bar for more of those two things before shuffling off in the direction of Hotel Katowice to rest up for the hockey-riffic days ahead.

I had hoped to wake at the crack of dawn and go for a vigorous, maybe even killer run around Katowice the following morning, but jet leg had its way with me and I instead slept until around eleven before dragging myself out of bed in search of coffee. As I strolled around downtown Katowice, it occurred to me that the city was not unlike my native Cleveland, only perhaps a bit colder and with a slightly more complicated history—you know, cuz of World War II, postwar communism, and other historically negative things. And while realizing this made me feel instantly a bit more at home, it also occurred to me that I was the new guy in town, sort of like a detective on some old TV drama who shows up to ask the locals the tough questions even though most of mine have to do with hockey and snacks. This realization put a little spring in my step, and I used it to duck inside an antique shop in search of ancient—or at least slightly dusty—Polish treasures.

I wasn't in the Polish antique shop a minute before I hit pay dirt in the form of a small plastic pin with a hockey goalie on it that said KATOWICE 1976. Considering that I had flown all the way to Katowice for the primary purpose of meeting up with a hockey goalie, you'll understand when I tell you how I was practically vibrating with excitement at the discovery of this particular pin. I instantly marched it to the register, paid five zloty* for it and continued on my way.

I'd made plans to meet up with Al at my hotel that afternoon and grab lunch in the neighborhood. He was already familiar with the Hotel Katowice, as it turned out he lived directly across the street in a colossal apartment complex along with a couple of his Naprzód Janów teammates.

I stepped out of the elevator to find Al in the lobby, dressed in a black pea coat, sweater and jeans. He's twenty-six and built like a guy who plays pro hockey in Poland, which is to say in better shape than me, even though I had already walked at least five hundred yards that morning. We walked a few blocks and grabbed a table at an Italian place in the town square. I was impressed when Al spoke Polish to the waitress as soon as she came over.

"You're fluent in Polish?" I asked him.

"No," he replied. "But I started picking it up pretty quickly after I got here this past summer."

I didn't have the heart to tell him that after two visits to Poland so far, I still only knew the words for beer and fries and was already a person of interest to local authorities. Unfortunately, the menu was in Polish, too, so I figured I might be stuck ordering beer and fries again, since they were the only two things I

---

* About $1.25.

recognized at first until I spotted the words *margherita pizza*, which I guess is the same in English and Polish, and told the waitress I wanted that instead immediately after Al ordered some pasta dish that was called something else in Polish.

"How did you wind up here in Poland?" I asked Al, getting the obvious question out of the way as soon as our waitress left.

"I got an opportunity to come play for Naprzód Janów through my agent, and then ended up getting a two-way deal to play for GKS Katowice, too," he told me.

As part of his deal, Al starts in goal for Naprzód Janów while also practicing regularly with GKS Katowice as one of their backup goalies. Given my childhood dream of becoming a pro hockey player, I was at first doubly jealous of the fact that Al managed to do it not once but twice at the same time, but then I remembered how we were technically related, at least as far as I was concerned, and I was just happy for him.

Al got his start playing hockey on his family's backyard pond in New Haven, Connecticut.

"I was really into the equipment," he explained. "So I became a goalie when I was five."

I can't imagine agreeing to let people shoot pucks at me at that age—or even now, the more I think about it. But it seems Al knew what he was doing as things progressed quickly for him. By his teenage years, he was playing in the United States Premier Hockey League for the Portland Junior Pirates before moving on to the Springfield Junior Pics. From there, he headed north to Canada to play a couple seasons in the Northern Ontario Junior Hockey League, spending time minding the net for the Elliot Lake Wildcats, French River Rapids and Timmins Rock.

"Did you billet with families in Canada?" I asked him, excited I finally had an opportunity to use the word *billet* in a sentence, as I've only ever seen or heard it used in the context of Canadian junior hockey players living away from home with families where their team is located, and I have sadly lived a life where talk of where Canadian junior hockey players sleep just hasn't happened enough.

"Yeah," Al told me.

I did my best to hide my envy by nodding politely while stuffing a slice of pizza into my face as soon as our food arrived.

From Canadian juniors, Al moved on to play NCAA Division III hockey at St. Mary's University of Minnesota, something you'd think my brother and his wife would have mentioned to me at least once at Thanksgiving or something, but no. The important thing, though, is that whatever efforts my brother and his wife might have put forth to keep Al's hockey career— and indeed, his very existence—a secret from me had failed miserably, as evidenced by the fact that I was now sitting across from him at a restaurant in Poland and they weren't.

"The hockey fans here are pretty intense," Al warned me. "Almost like British soccer hooligans."

And since, up until recently, GKS Katowice and KS Katowice Naprzód Janów both played in the Polish Hockey League, the rivalry between the two teams and their respective fans remains intense.

"Right after I got into town this past summer," Al told me,

"I was waiting for the bus while wearing a shirt with a Naprzód logo on it and a GKS Katowice fan came right up to me and spit on my chest."

"But you're on the GKS Katowice team, too!" I said.

"He didn't know that," Al shrugged.

I felt bad for Al while also kind of admiring his assailant's enthusiasm.

As long as I was now vicariously enjoying Al's hockey career, random hockey fan attacks and all, I figured I'd just go ahead and project my boyhood dreams onto him and ask if he might play in the NHL one day.

"I'm definitely interested," he told me, "but hockey isn't the only thing I'm interested in, so we'll see."

It's at this point that I wanted to tell him that I really, really needed him to play in the NHL so he could live out my dreams and I could then also tell anyone who would listen that I know him, but I decided to play it cool and instead focus on having my way with the rest of the pizza.

After lunch, Al walked me back to Hotel Katowice. Along the way, we passed about a dozen young men decked out from head to toe in GKS Katowice gear, presumably in anticipation of tonight's home game against Kraków. Almost on cue, one of them threw his shoulder into Al's, presumably looking to start a fight with the two of us—a death wish, I choose to believe, even though I've never been in a street fight in my life.

"See what I mean?" Al said to me.

I was relieved that Al kept his cool and didn't retaliate, since the last thing I felt like doing after eating all that pizza was to kick twelve dudes' asses without even really trying. Instead we just kept walking to the hotel, while I resisted the urge to tell Al he should just wear his GKS Katowice jersey at all times to avoid further incident. Then I gave him the pin with the goalie on it I'd bought earlier in hopes it might give him a little extra protection on the mean streets of Katowice.

"I've met this guy," Al said, looking at the pin.

"That's a real guy?" I asked.

"Yeah, it's Andrzej Tkacz," Al replied. "He played for Katowice in the seventies."

Best five zloty I ever spent.

Still jet-lagged, I decided to take a nap once I got up to my room, only to be woken up throughout by the chanting of what, of course, turned out to be GKS Katowice fans out on the street, getting pumped for that night's game against Comarch Cracovia, aka Kraków. Normally this might annoy me, but in this case it was like sweet music to my ears, as I was thrilled to be joining them for the game in a few hours while Al was across town, practicing with Naprzód Janów again ahead of their two games this weekend. I also made a mental note to leave behind in my room the Quebec Nordiques hat I'd brought with me, in the event that the GKS fans liked to hand out beatings to anyone wearing hockey paraphernalia not associated with their team.

"Officers, it's Dave, the guy who struggles to use crosswalks in accordance with local ordinances," I imagined myself saying to the local police had I committed to the Nordiques hat and gotten what I deserved. "I've been burned by my love of the Šťastný brothers again."

I headed to the Spodek Arena a bit before game time in hopes of catching the fans getting up to their antics before the opening face-off. It turns out Spodek is Polish for "saucer," which makes sense, as the arena from afar looks like something out of *The Jetsons*.

As I approached the entrance to the arena, I had the distinct feeling that I was being sized up by the groups of fans huddled outside, smoking and giving off a general air of hockeycentric menace. Regardless of whether it was true or not, I liked the idea that they might view me as some sort of threat, a guy who might need to be dealt with, and fast. Still, in the interest of avoiding further conflict, I made a point of buying a GKS Katowice hat and pulling it onto my head just as soon as I got inside.

My original plan was to embed myself with the rowdiest of GKS fans and, who knows, maybe even take my shirt off while flipping off the entire Kraków bench and a couple other folks who didn't deserve it whatsoever. But, owing to my delicate features, I imagine, I was instead ushered to sit with the older, seemingly more family-oriented and presumably less violent fans on the side of the ice opposite the thousand or so black, green and yellow clad GKS fans, who were already chanting in Polish that I didn't understand a word of but have no doubt was absolutely awesome. I decided to console myself with a large Okocim beer paired with a bottled water so that I might stay properly hydrated throughout the first period.

In between the pregame warm-up and the opening face-off, some young children and the GKS Katowice mascot—who was not an animal or some mythical being as you might expect, but instead appeared to be just some guy with a giant head who dressed like he worked in customer service somewhere—skated around the rink with various flags I didn't recognize. In a perfect world, I would have been out there skating around with them, but it had already become clear to me that things weren't going entirely my way tonight.

"Get off the ice, assholes," I yelled. "We got a hockey game to play."

It's amazing what you're capable of once you decide no one around you can understand a word you're saying.

A couple minutes later, the game was underway and—thanks in part to the beer, I'm guessing—I found myself screaming along with everyone else in attendance almost immediately. I was also instantly struck by the fluid nature of the European version of hockey. As rumored, it's a less physical game than in North America, where rinks are smaller and assorted violence, both sanctioned and otherwise, is more frequent. I've always found finesse more exciting than, say, a winger being clothes-lined out at the blue line, so this was just fine by me. The GKS hooligans across the ice from me seemed fine with it, too, as their cheers remained relentless. Even so, it wasn't quite enough, as the first period ended with Kraków up 1–0.

As I sought further liquid sustenance and what appeared to be half of the people in attendance stepped outside for a smoke, I was delighted to hear that GKS superfans continue their chanting throughout the entire first intermission. In fact, from where I was standing in the beer line, it sounded as if the game might still be underway. The GKS fans' near-violent enthusiasm was infectious, too; by the time the second period began, I pretty much felt like I'd been a GKS Katowice diehard my entire life. In fact, I can say with certainty I was having more fun than I had ever had at a sporting event in my life before. And who cares if I came to the game all by myself—the intensity of the fans made it feel like we were all there together, regardless of the fact that I'd wandered in off the streets all alone like some sort of weirdo who'd rolled into town from New York just the day before. And, no doubt adding to the good vibes, my ticket, three beers and three bottled waters I drank over the course of the game cost me less than twenty dollars total.

"Pack your things," I texted my girlfriend, Kathy, upon this realization. "We're moving to the eleventh-largest city in Poland!"

I can't say for sure how much my own personal cheering helped turn the tide for GKS Katowice that night, but they tied things up 1–1 by the end of the second period and ultimately destroyed those chumps from Kraków, 4–1, including one empty-net goal toward the end of the game after Kraków pulled their goalie in an act of desperation I have seen pay off almost never during my time here on earth.

Considering the fact that, up until just a few weeks prior to my trip, I had never even heard of the GKS Katowice team, I was surprised at how happy their win made me feel as I walked in the direction of my hotel after the game. I was pretty much ready to set cars on fire. Still, given my run-in with local law enforcement the night before, I instead decided to celebrate the win by grabbing dinner at a Vietnamese place called A Dong Restaurant near my hotel that I had spotted earlier in the day and made a mental note to return to for obvious and admittedly juvenile reasons.

I woke the following morning and hit up a neighborhood coffee shop for a breakfast that consisted of a peanut butter and beet sandwich that wasn't nearly as disgusting as it sounds and a cappuccino. Today was Saturday, and Naprzód Janów was playing an early evening game against MMKS Podhale Nowy Targ, a team from a couple hours southeast of Katowice.

Naprzód Janów plays in a rink located in a part of town called Nikiszowiec, a former coal miners' settlement complete with large *familoks*, a word I just learned that means multifamily residences, directly across from the arena. Al had recommended I take a bus the three or so miles to the arena from my hotel, but I was feeling adventurous, so I decided to walk, assuming I'd happen upon countless local delights and, who knows, maybe even be invited inside some friendly stranger's home for cabbage rolls and cider along the way. I was mistaken, however, as the most exciting thing I encountered on my journey was a Pizza Hut Express, located just outside of Katowice proper, that appeared to be closed. The rest of the walk involved me alternately shuffling through the woods or trudging alongside a highway with almost no other humans in sight aside from those zipping past in cars. At one point, after at least an hour of walking in the cold, it started to snow and I began to contemplate all my life choices and what had got me here, walking all alone, seemingly in the middle of nowhere in Poland in the dead of winter. My mind ping-ponged between opposite conclusions that my life was either completely amazing or an absolute mess.

Shortly after that, I began to feel as if I were in a bleak, presumably Polish, foreign film where the guy from out of town is brutally murdered in the middle of the woods, his body covered entirely in fresh snowfall in a matter of minutes. And while, yes, I realize I have alluded to my own murder at least twice already in this chapter, if you've ever visited Poland in February, you're no doubt impressed with my restraint in not mentioning it at least a few more times by now.

I was relieved to emerge from the woods still very much alive a short while later. And after a brief stroll through Nikiszowiec proper, during which I stopped off for a slice of blueberry coffee cake and a cappuccino as if I hadn't just been having an existential crisis all alone in the woods just minutes before, I headed inside the Naprzód Janów home arena just across the street from the *familoks*, where I promptly removed my Nordiques hat and replaced it with the Naprzód Janów hat I bought at the concession stand just in case the fans of the home team were anything like the GKS Katowice fans.

Al had warned me that, unlike the GKS Katowice's home ice at Spodek, the Naprzód Janów arena was still under Covid restrictions, so attendance would be capped at around three hundred people. I assumed this meant today's game would be a relatively low-key affair. And when I also learned that there was no alcohol for sale at the arena, I was certain of it. But I couldn't have been more wrong, as, despite their smaller number, the crowd at the Naprzód Janów was even more fired up than the one at the GKS Katowice game the night before. Even better, I was able to sit with the hooligans and at least pretend to join them in their chanting, even though I had no idea what they were saying.

As the players from Naprzód Janów and MMKS Podhale Nowy Targ took the ice, I noticed that it seemed only the players from Podhale, as I learned they are called for short, touched the ice before doing the sign of the cross on themselves. And being on the right side of the Lord seemed to work for them, too, as Podhale scored the first goal of the game. Granted, from where I was sitting, it looked like they scored as a result of an error on the part of the Naprzód Janów defense, who didn't give my distant relative Al Rogers the support he needed in the goal crease, but, being raised Catholic and all, I figure the sign of the cross couldn't have hurt.

While I continued to try to blend in with the Naprzód Janów hooligans, it occurred to me that it was the first time I'd seen a family member, however distant, play in a sporting event since at least high school. And from there, my mind somehow drifted back to about third grade, when I was playing on the school soccer team and one of my uncles came out to watch a game one Saturday morning. I remember being so excited that he was there and wanting to make him proud despite the fact that I was horrible at soccer and spent most of my time on the field praying the ball would never actually come to me. Even so, I was still hoping for some sort of praise from my uncle after the game.

"Well . . . ," he said, seemingly struggling for words as I approached him afterward, "I see you played."

It was a quiet ride home. And while I can't imagine Al gave a crap one way or another what I thought about him and his team, what with his being a grown man and all, I found our familial connection, however distant, had me invested in the game a bit more than I might normally have been. And as such, I was determined to be able to give him a better postgame review than I got from my uncle all those years ago. So, when the second period ended with Naprzód Janów ahead, 4–3, I was absolutely thrilled, so much in fact that I decided to treat myself to a hot chocolate at the concession stand before quickly rejoining the hooligans in screaming in the stands.

As if things weren't exciting enough, at some point during the third period of the game, what appeared to be a high school girls' track team wandered into the arena and began cheering while continuing to run in place, which just goes to show you anything goes at a Polish hockey game. And while I'll go to my grave wondering exactly how and why a girls' track team showed up out of nowhere like that, it certainly didn't hurt matters, as the game ended with Naprzód Janów winning, 5–3.

I don't know if it was the stress of wanting my distant relative Al to get the win that day, the jet lag, the fact I was having a completely amazing time all by myself in Poland, or perhaps some combination of all three of those things, but Naprzód Janów's victory that day moved me almost to tears.

"This is awesome," I thought as my eyes began to well up ever so slightly. "I'm actually capable of human emotion after all!"

Since Naprzód Janów had another game to play the next afternoon, I figured Al needed to rest up. So, rather than pestering him to see if he wanted to destroy public property with me in celebration of the team's victory that day, I instead decided to contain myself, quietly exit the arena and catch a bus back into town, where I celebrated the victory by going back to the Italian restaurant Al and I had lunch at the day before and inhaling another margherita pizza with a couple glasses of red wine while watching an elderly drunken man scream and dance all alone at the bar before eventually wandering over to my table, looking to make a little conversation.

"English," I said sheepishly in between bites of pizza as he continued speaking to me in Polish anyway, as though I not only understood exactly what he was saying but was also enjoying it very much.

After a couple minutes, he wandered back over to his spot at the bar to continue screaming and dancing all alone for a while before being escorted away by police, a reminder that some-times it really is best to keep your emotions inside.

I woke early the next day, as Naprzód Janów had a Sunday home game against UKS Bears Mosir Sanok at the ungodly hour of noon, which, considering that I'd arrived from New York City just a few days before, still pretty much felt like 6 a.m. to my weary bones. Even so, given the fun I'd had watching hockey games the past couple nights, I couldn't wait to get over to the rink and continue with my wannabe hooligan ways.

While I probably could have used the exercise, I decided to treat myself and take the bus over to the arena this time. As it turned out, the bus stopped directly in front of my hotel and, aside from my diversion through the woods, took almost the exact same route to get the rink as I'd walked the day before, finally dropping me off right in front of the arena. This realization made me feel a little stupid about walking all that way the day before, but I still felt pretty good about cheating death like that.

Since this was my second day in a row at the Naprzód Janów home arena, I was starting to feel like a regular. So, after pulling my team hat onto my head, I walked inside, grabbed a hot chocolate and headed straight for my perch among the local hooligans. But as the game got underway that afternoon, the hooligans, who'd been absolutely insane the night before, were weirdly quiet. As it turned out, their drummer was just late. So, after that bastard finally straggled in a few minutes later, the nonstop chanting was underway once more.

One big difference between the GKS Katowice Polish Hockey League game and the Naprzód Janów Polish 1. Liga games is that a lot more players in the Polish 1. Liga wear face masks. This, it turns out, is because the Polish 1. Liga allows players under the age of eighteen, and they are required to wear cages with their helmets.

"Some older guys still wear cages," Al explained to me, "but those guys are weirdos."

Like the other two Polish hockey games I'd already seen, today's was especially fast and not very physical, aside from a second-period hooking penalty against Naprzód Janów for which UKS Bears Mosir Sanok were awarded a penalty shot that they ended up blowing, much to the delight of me and my fellow hooligans. When the Bears scored a breakaway goal shortly after, though, I was none too pleased and let loose with a string of expletives, much to both my own surprise and the surprise of a mother sitting nearby with her approximately four-year-old son. I immediately tried to plug the word *sorry* into my phone app, but they had already moved away from me by the time I was able to pull it up. Even so, I was still impressed both by my capacity for enthusiasm at a day game like that and a Polish mother's ability to understand English profanity so well.

In the end, Naprzód Janów made light work of UKS Bears Mosir Sanok, defeating them 6–3, after which the Naprzód Janów players stayed on the ice for what had quickly become my favorite part of Polish hockey games: when the home team lines up in front of the hooligans and they trade chants I will never understand in a million years, seemingly to both celebrate and thank each other for the win. It gives the feeling that the players and fans are all just one team. Even cooler is that Naprzód Janów is actually a sports club comprising both a hockey team and a soccer team, so it turns out the club's fans show up to support both teams regardless of their interest in a particular sport.

"Some of the hooligans don't even understand hockey at all," Al told me. "They just come to support Naprzód Janów regardless."

I met Al in the lobby of the arena after the game and we walked over to take the bus back into town together. Along the way, he pointed out some GKS Katowice graffiti on the walls opposite the Naprzód Janów arena.

"Back when the two teams played against each other," Al told me, "there would be brawls in the street out here between the fans of both teams."

I'm no fan of violence, but as hinted at previously, I do love enthusiasm, so the idea that fans of two teams that both represent the same city would get together and beat the crap out of each other absolutely tickled me.

Al and I arrived at the bus stop to find his teammates and roommates, twenty-five-year-old American center Mike Thamert and twenty-three-year-old Australian defenseman Bayley Kubara, respectively the number two and three scorers on the team, already there waiting. As we hopped on the bus together, I thought about how cool it was that pro hockey players would just hop on a city bus home after a victory, especially since that victory involved Mike scoring the best goal of the game—he weaved between two opposing defensemen to glide across the goal crease and rifle the puck over the UKS Bears Mosir Sanok goalie's shoulder and into the net. It made me wonder if any of the New York Rangers have ever just grabbed the A train home after a game at Madison Square Garden. Professional athletes—they're just like us, I guess.

"I didn't even realize they had hockey in Australia," I told Bayley as we cruised back into town.

"Yup," he replied, presumably tired of people like me saying things like that.

"Bayley's one of the best hockey players in all of Australia," Al added. And since Australia winter happens during Polish summer, Bayley goes home to play pro hockey in Australia at the end of the Polish season. To be honest, when I learned this, I started to get annoyed at how almost everyone I met during my trip to Poland played for more than one pro hockey team. And when I remembered that Mike played for only one pro hockey team, I thought about giving him crap about it to distract from the reality that I was the only non—pro hockey player sitting in the back of the bus that day. In the end, though, I decided against it and instead made plans to meet all three of them for dinner later.

After a quick stop back at the hotel to give my relentless jet lag a stern talking to, I met up with Al, Bayley and Mike in front of Hotel Katowice and we headed over to the Italian place where I was starting to feel like a regular—and, yes, I ate another one of those margherita pizzas all by myself like some goddamn animal. Over a few beers, we chatted about hockey and life in Poland.

"It can be a strange place," Al said. "Every day there seems to be another 'What the fuck?' moment."

"What do you mean?" I asked.

"Just something happens that makes absolutely no sense," Al continued as Bayley and Mike nodded in agreement. At first, I had no idea what Al meant, but then my mind began to drift back to a couple days earlier, when it seemed like I was about to go to jail for crossing the street against the crosswalk signal.

"Yeah," I said. "I could see that."

Later that night, Al gave me a tour of Mariacka Street, the main drag in town full of lively bars and restaurants and other things people who think they are going to live forever tend to gravitate toward. It's also a pedestrians-only street, which was nice because it gave me a chance to finally relax and not worry about being hassled by the local police while walking. After a few blocks, we stopped into a bar for a nightcap and more hockey talk. And since I'd had a few by this point, I couldn't stop myself from being more vocal about wanting Al to live out my hockey dreams for me.

"So, are you gonna play hockey here next year?" I asked him.

"I'm not sure yet," Al replied.

"I think you should," I told him. "And then go play in the NHL."

"We'll see," Al said, politely putting up with my bullshit.

"You should do it! Play in the NHL!" I slurred before realizing this is exactly the kind of behavior that would make my brother and his wife regret ever telling me Al existed in the first place.

Our drinks finished, Al and I left the bar and walked back to his place, where we were to meet up with his friend Alex Yakimenko, a twenty-five-year-old defenseman for the GKS Katowice team.

"Be on the lookout for a bowlegged Estonian," Al said to me on the way over.

As if on cue, Alex, who is from Estonia and bowlegged, appeared in front of us, having just gotten back into town after an away game that day against KH Energa Toruń, a team located about four hours north of Katowice. The three of us headed up to Al's place, where Bayley and Mike were already relaxing.

When we got upstairs, I told Alex how I felt like the GKS Katowice fans were sizing me up outside the arena before the game a couple nights earlier.

"They were totally sizing you up," Alex told me.

It felt good to have Alex confirm my suspicions that I was dangerous like that.

"Alex has been moving around, playing for different teams around Europe since he was thirteen," Al told me.

A quick look at Al's, Alex's, Mike's and Bayley's pages on eliteprospects.com, a website where you can keep tabs on the career stats of seemingly every pro or semipro hockey player on earth, reveals that they all have that in common—moving from city to city, state to state and country to country in the name of hockey. And when I considered that for a moment, it suddenly dawned on me that even though I never traveled more than a few suburbs away to play hockey, we still had a lot in common as we were all ramblin' men, if I may borrow from the Allman Brothers and the great Hank Williams before them. And on this cold night in February, our rambling had led us to all be sitting in this cramped apartment, late at night in Katowice, Poland, while talking about the greatest game on earth. And at the time, that felt like pure magic to me.

I had an early flight back to New York via Warsaw the next morning, so I said my goodbyes and headed off in the direction of Hotel Katowice once more. It was past midnight and there wasn't a car in sight. Still, before I crossed the street, I stood there waiting momentarily for the crosswalk signal to change from red to green so as to avoid trouble from the local authorities. Then suddenly I just decided to boldly cross the street against the signal anyway and just walk right into my hotel like a man who's not afraid to die.

Let's see those chumps from Kraków try that shit.

3

Slava Fetisov and Me: The Oneness

It wasn't easy being a hockey fan in Cleveland, Ohio, way back in the seventies. First, the WHA's Cleveland Crusaders, not wanting to compete for fans with the incoming Cleveland Barons, skipped town in 1976, sweet purple jerseys and all, to become the Minneapolis Fighting Saints after just four seasons in the Paris of Northeast Ohio. Meanwhile, the Cleveland Barons, who had arrived on the scene the following season to ostensibly give Clevelanders a taste of some of that scorching-hot NHL action they'd been waiting for their whole lives, just stuck the knife in further, pulling the exact same move by merging with the Minnesota North Stars after just two not-exactly-amazing seasons. It was a lot to take for local hockey fans, but as best I could tell, not many other people seemed to notice, or at least not that many other kids at my elementary school.

"Did you hear the Barons are leaving town?" I'd ask a schoolmate out on the playground.

"Shut up and give me your lunch money, Hill!" they'd reply.

It may not have gone down exactly like that, and let's be clear, the lunch money was never handed over, mostly because I never carried cash and tended to go home for lunch most days anyway, but hopefully you see my point.

The Barons only managed to fill even half of the Richfield Coliseum* and draw more than ten thousand fans to any of their home games on a handful of occasions during their time in town. And while, generally speaking, I wasn't exactly helping the situation, what with being a kid without money or a car and all, the important thing is that, at at least one of those games, a young Dave Hill was very much in attendance.

I'd be lying if I said I remember who the Barons were playing that night, but I do know that my Canadian grandfather,** my dad, my mother, my brother Bob and I somehow found ourselves seated directly behind the penalty box, which felt fancy since neither my grandfather nor my

---

* Conveniently located not in Cleveland itself, but instead just twenty-odd miles outside the city in the middle of—with all due respect to local residents—nowhere.

** For further discussion on my grandfather and his Canadianness, please refer to my previous book *Parking the Moose*, a timeless literary classic.

dad were ones to splurge very often, and just pulling into the arena parking lot probably would have been thrilling enough for the six-year-old me. My best guess is that my grandfather, a haberdasher, scored the tickets in exchange for giving some-one a good deal on a bulk purchase of golf sweaters or some-thing. However it happened, I was now suddenly sitting mere feet away from these giant beskated* men, almost all of whom seemed to have—in accordance with the unwritten rule of 1970s professional hockey—wavy hair and impossibly thick mustaches, playing the sport of the gods.

It was my first time seeing anyone other than children play hockey in person, and the whole night seemed to be in Techni-color. My most vivid memory, though, was when Barons defense-man Len Frig served a two-minute minor directly in front of us before leaping back onto the ice mid-play, no doubt to continue handing out his own brand of swift justice. The fact that it hap-pened directly in front of me was enough to instantly make Frig my favorite hockey player.** Sometimes proximity is all it takes.

While Len and the rest of the Barons left Cleveland for icier pastures*** not long after that fateful night, the experience was

---

* A word I just made up but stand by its efficacy.

** With all due respect to Mr. Frig, I have changed "favorite players" roughly four thousand times since then, but that doesn't change the fact that I have an eight-by-ten glossy of the man hanging in my bathroom at this very moment and have zero plans of ever removing it.

*** Len himself went on to play for the St. Louis Blues the following season. And prior to playing for the Cleveland Barons, Len played for two seasons still somehow enough to convince me I was the foremost ice hockey authority in my entire parish—at the very least—as I had finally witnessed the blinding speed and fury of the world's greatest game up close and in person. The problem, of course, was that there was no longer a pro hockey team in my town and it would still be years before we got cable TV and grainy transmissions of *Hockey Night in Canada* began making their way to our living room from this magical land up north, where hockey games on TV weren't the exception but business as usual. So, for a time, aside from quietly scanning the NHL standings in the sports section of the *Cleveland Plain Dealer* before trying to make sense of the myriad of massage parlor ads* that flanked them, I had little choice but to just be some weird kid mumbling to himself about a sport almost no one else at school cared about.

———————————

with the NHL's short-lived California Golden Seals, something I only bring up to highlight that I'm guessing it must have sounded awkward for the Seals' opponents to have to talk about "beating the Seals." On the flip side, it would have been fun to hear an opposing team's fans talk about having been "beaten by the Seals" after a particularly tough defeat, as out of context it might sound like they were discussing a particularly harrowing trip to the beach, where the tables were turned. I guess this is probably as good a time as any to tell you that these footnotes are strictly bonus content and nothing you've been at all charged for when purchasing this book. They are simply my gift to you.

* I probably shouldn't be getting into this, but yes, they were *that* kind of massage parlor, not that I realized it at the time. I just figured there was something about sports that rendered grown-ups tense and exhausted, and the local massage establishments were trying to help.

"Did you know that you can't play the puck if one or both feet are still in the penalty box?" I'd ask a schoolmate out on the playground.

"Huh?" they'd grunt back.

"Nothing," I'd reply. "I was just saying how phonics is bullshit."

All of that changed, of course, in 1980, when the Winter Olympics came to Lake Placid, New York, and against all odds the United States men's hockey team won the gold medal. Suddenly, if only for a few short, glorious weeks, hockey was America's favorite sport. If you weren't around at the time, let me just say it was not unlike 2018, when the United States Olympic curling team defeated Canada to win the gold medal and all anyone in America could talk about for at least the next three or four hours was curling, but, you know, much, much bigger, thanks in no small part to the fact that we had beaten the Soviet Union's national team to do it.

I wasn't old enough to realize that the United States playing hockey against the Soviet Union was essentially the Cold War on ice, and I'm now a bit jealous about how much that must have added to the entertainment for any world-affairs buffs who happened to be tuning in. I just remember that we were supposed to absolutely hate the Soviet team for reasons the young Dave failed to fully comprehend.

"We better beat those Soviet bastards," someone might casually remark at the barbershop or deli down the street from my house in an attempt to fill the air.

"Yes," I'd agree, just trying to fit in, "the bastards of the Soviet Union must be defeated."

Still, deep down inside, I just couldn't make the idea stick.

"After all," I thought, "how bad could these Soviet guys be if they play my favorite sport?"

What I did understand, however, was that the Soviet players were scary as hell. While the United States players looked like a bunch of kids—even team captain Mike Eruzione, who was already a grizzled twenty-five-year-old and therefore pretty much staring at the grave as far as I was concerned—the Soviet players looked like a bunch of grown men. Men who had secrets, played knife games at breakfast and wrestled bears just to break up the day a little bit. To even watch them from the comfort of my family's home felt unsafe.

"What's to stop Vladislav Tretiak from just coming to my house and kicking my ass right into the next yard?" I wondered. All these years later, it's still hard not to worry about it at least a little bit.

My fears aside, however, what was so amazing about the United States defeating the Soviet Union was that the Soviets had, by all sane accounts, a much better hockey team. For starters, they'd won the gold medal in five of the six previous Winter Olympic Games, and I can only assume that they lost on purpose as some sort of weird character-building exercise cooked up by their authoritarian coach, Viktor Tikhonov. And unlike the United States hockey team, which was mostly made up of guys who hadn't played past the college level, the Soviet team was mostly ringers, professional players like Tretiak—widely considered to be the best goalie on the planet at the time—who had already beaten the crap out of teams all over the world and had shown up in Lake Placid presumably just to toy with everybody for a couple weeks before heading home to laugh about the whole thing while guzzling vodka straight from the bottle and holding open flames under his hands for a really long time without so much as blinking.

Keeping all this in mind, I was absolutely thrilled that the United States won the gold that year. In fact, the win is almost entirely responsible for inspiring me to finally make the leap from just playing hockey out in the driveway to actually joining the local youth league the following season. Still, my awe of the Soviet national hockey team has remained ever since. So, when my friend Jim casually mentioned that he actually knew Slava Fetisov—one of the greatest defensemen ever to play the game, and who, along with Tretiak, forwards Boris Mikhailov, Valeri Kharlamov and Vladimir Petrov, and defenseman Alexei Kasatonov, made up the starting lineup of the Soviet team at Lake Placid—I not so casually asked if he might put us in touch.

"Call him, Jim," I said. "Call him right now!"

"Calm down, Dave," Jim replied. "I'll email him tomorrow."

As it turned out, Jim had met Fetisov while working on *Red Army*, an excellent documentary you should definitely see if you haven't already. It's about the Soviet national hockey team and is told mostly from Fetisov's perspective. And even though Jim assured me that Fetisov is every bit as warm and thoughtful as he comes across in the film, and despite the fact that he is now in his sixties and I am now a grown man who can run fast and lift heavy things when necessary, I was still a bit intimidated at the idea of speaking with him over Zoom a few days later. The very idea of it instantly had me feeling like that kid who watched him on TV at the Lake Placid Olympics all those years ago.

"What's to stop Fetisov from just coming to my house and kicking my ass right into the next yard?" I wondered.

I tried not to let that thought mess with my head too much as I sat down in front of my laptop to connect with him on his phone while he sat in the back of a car slowly rolling through what appeared to be a pitch-black Moscow. Instead, I just reminded myself that I was a grown man with much to be proud of in this life, and if at any point during my conversation with Fetisov I felt in over my head or anything, I could just shut my laptop without warning and act as if none of this had ever happened.

"So," I began, digging into my list of hard-hitting questions Fetisov would never see coming, "how important is the sport of hockey in Russia?"

"It is the number one game," he told me. "We couldn't be thankful enough to the Canadians for inventing it."

Fetisov's answer didn't surprise me, but it still had me slightly fuming inside, as right up there with a lack of proper health care, economic inequality and weak gun laws on my list of complaints about America is the fact that hockey isn't nearly as popular as it should be here. And if Russia, located over six thousand kilometers from Canada, can manage to make hockey its number one sport, certainly the United States, located just down the street from Canada, relatively speaking, can at least get it in the top three.

What with Fetisov being one of the greatest ever to play the game of hockey and all, I assumed it was all hockey, all the time just as soon as the doctors had finished rinsing the placenta off him. But I was wrong.

"I played soccer, basketball, volleyball, all the different sports," he said of his youth. "Hockey was just one of the sports."

I honestly never saw the volleyball thing coming. But more than that, I was kind of annoyed by this answer, too, as hockey is the only sport I ever really tried to excel at. And given that I now make my way in the world writing books and stuff, well, you can see how that worked out. Then again, I guess that's how it goes with great athletes. Bo Jackson was an all-star in both football and baseball, Michael Jordan managed to squeeze in some time as a minor league baseball player before returning to the NBA, and even Wayne Gretzky supposedly once considered being a pro baseball player, which, if it had come to pass, would not only have changed the course of the entire game but would also pretty much guarantee I wouldn't have an Edmonton Oilers jersey in my laundry hamper right now. Oh, and you can also bet I never would have eaten at his since-closed Wayne Gretzky's restaurant in Toronto three times more than most people have, either.

One thing Fetisov and I did have in common despite our divergent careers is that we were both put on skates at an early age.

"My father put me on the skates when I was four," said Fetisov, who grew up in a poor community in Moscow. "They were double-bladed, attached to the shoes by ropes."

Fetisov moved on from double-bladed skates attached by ropes pretty quickly, becoming a Red Army school team member by the age of ten, one year younger than I was when I first stepped onto the ice as a Cleveland Heights house league player to launch a hockey career that, all these years later, only my father and I seem to remember much.

"I sure don't miss getting up so early to drive you to hockey practice," my dad will sometimes mention during a conversation about something else entirely.

"Me neither, Dad," I'll tell him. "Me neither."

Getting back to Fetisov, however—as you can probably imagine, his career took off a little faster than mine (so, rest assured, I will stop talking about mine at the end of this sentence—at least for the rest of this chapter, anyway. Maybe.). By 1973, at the age of fifteen, Fetisov was a member of the first Soviet junior team to play in Canada, where he competed against many of the same players he would later face in the NHL. Oh, and they beat everybody while they were at it.

"We didn't have any of the equipment you guys had, didn't have the sticks you guys had," Fetisov said, directly addressing the Canadians while staring ahead into traffic in a way that I found delightfully menacing, "but we beat everybody."

"Take that, Canada," I thought, quickly and momentarily siding with Russia in hopes of somehow ingratiating myself with Fetisov, whom I just chose to believe could read my mind.

You'd think there would have been a parade back in Moscow for Fetisov and his teammates after destroying everybody in the Canadian junior tournament like that, but no.

"It was not a big deal," Fetisov explained in a tone seemingly meant to calm me down. "It was just fifteen- and sixteen-year-old kids playing hockey in Canada."

At this point I decided to blow Fetisov away with both my knowledge of his career and my skill at pronouncing Russian names.

"How long after that did you start playing under Viktor Tikhonov on the national team?" I asked him.

"Nineteen seventy-seven," Fetisov told me. "But this was different coaches."

I was so embarrassed about getting my timeline of Soviet coaches wrong that I almost shut my laptop right then and there, despite—let the record show—nailing my pronunciation of Tikhonov's last name. But Fetisov took my error in stride.

"I was eighteen years old when I was debuting for the national team," he continued. "This was pretty young for a defenseman."

I'd heard some crazy stories about how hard the Soviet national team trained back then, how they all lived year-round together in barracks, played hockey all day and whipped kettle bells around like rag dolls.

"It was only an eleven-month stay, especially when you get older," Fetisov said of the barracks. "This was the standard to us back then."

"I can't even moisturize for eleven months straight," I thought to tell him before deciding to definitely not do that. Instead, I asked him how the Soviet national team's training differed from how hockey teams trained in the rest of the world at the time.

"I didn't know and I didn't care," Fetisov told me. "But anywhere we went in Europe and Canada and the United States, all these specialists would write down all these notes to see how we did our drills and how we played."

It was around this time in our conversation that Fetisov's car changed drivers in a way that made things seem even cooler and weirdly more Russian on his end of the Zoom session that I can't quite put my finger on. Regardless, as I sat at my kitchen table nine hours behind him in track pants and a T-shirt, I was kind of jealous. Instead of asking him about that, though, I asked him what I've been wondering ever since I was a kid watching him on TV at the 1980 Winter Olympics.

"Did you guys know that everyone in America was just in awe of you guys at Lake Placid?" I asked him. "I mean, I personally was terrified."

"But that's the beauty of the sport—a miracle can happen at any time," Fetisov said almost wistfully, focusing on the heart of the matter rather than my mostly irrational fears. "America beat us, who were almost unbeatable in every possible level."

Fetisov paused to let that sink in for a moment before reminding me how the Soviet Union beat Canada, 8–1, in the final of the 1981 Canada Cup.

"Never underestimate your opponent," he added, his Russian accent somehow adding to the gravity of those words, probably because I've seen one too many movies where there is a Russian guy who at least tries to kill someone at some point in the film.

Fetisov's hockey career would have been amazing enough had he never played beyond the Soviet national team. But he made history by coming to America to play in the NHL after that, no small feat considering that even bringing up the subject with the Soviet government in the first place was met with a demand from the minister of defense, Marshal Dmitry Yazov, to either apologize or be sent to Siberia, a generally negative place based on just about everything I've ever heard about it.

"The Soviet system wanted to sell me to the NHL," Fetisov recalled. "They tried to sell me as a slave to get my money and pay me around a thousand bucks a month."

Fetisov instead held out to sign a deal directly with the New Jersey Devils rather than having the Soviet Union government involved, a move that would not only pave the way for other Russian players to come to the NHL but would create opportunities for Russians in every field to work outside their home country.

"I opened the door and window for everybody," Fetisov said with understandable pride.

In 1989, Fetisov finally made his debut with the Devils at the age of thirty-one, almost a decade after NHL scouts had begun sniffing around.

"I came from the best team to play for the worst team in the league," Fetisov remembered.

And as if being in New Jersey weren't bad enough, his arrival was met with resistance from fans and the media who either didn't know or didn't care what he had gone through to get to the NHL.

"They said, 'Why is this communist coming here to take our money, blah, blah, blah,'" Fetisov said with a sigh. "But I had two choices—to go back to the Soviet Union or fight through and gain respect and be part of the National Hockey League."

It kind of reminded me of how my upperclassman hockey teammates in high school used to steal my towel when I was just a freshman, in hopes of breaking me. That which doesn't kill us only makes us stronger, I guess. And no one knows that better than Fetisov and me, as best I can tell.

Anyway, in 1995, Fetisov was traded to the Detroit Red Wings, where he was reunited with fellow Soviet national team players Sergei Fedorov, Vladimir Konstantinov, Slava Kozlov and Igor Larionov, collectively known as the Russian Five. Together with their teammates, they'd win back-to-back Stanley Cups in 1997 and 1998, after which Fetisov took the Stanley Cup to Moscow for its first visit ever. Then he headed back to New Jersey to be an assistant coach with the Devils for four years before returning home to Russia to begin his political career as the minister of sport—and, of course, continue his involvement with hockey.

Despite Fetisov's myriad accomplishments both on and off the ice—and, well, me being me—as I spoke with him it was hard not to feel like I'd met a kindred spirit, one of those rare people who get the magic of hockey at least as well as I do, so I asked him why hockey isn't more popular in America. "Surely he'll have the answer," I thought.

"I don't know," Fetisov said. "I still ask myself why Great Britain isn't a hockey country, because they like the rough and tough sports like rugby, but there's no hockey program."

It was at this point that I broke down and told him how hard it was being a kid growing up in Cleveland who loved hockey more than anything else and would actually get depressed when a football game even came on TV, a condition at least a couple relatives thought required medical attention.

"You're not a typical American," Slava mused. "You go against the grain, like me."

My inner ten-year-old perked up at that last line and I momentarily considered tracking down all my old schoolmates to tell them how much Slava Fetisov and I had in common and how they could all go straight to hell. But then Slava and I got to chatting some more, and I realized I can't be bothered with any of those bastards, anyway. Besides, I'm a gentleman.

Fetisov still plays hockey five or six days a week and also runs a hockey school called the Fetisov Hockey Academy, attended primarily by Russian children but soon also by one middle-aged man from Cleveland, if God exists.

"You still skate?" Fetisov asked me as our conversation was winding down.

"Not as much as I'd like," I said, my head down in shame.

"You should find the time, you know," Fetisov replied.

Part of me wanted him to threaten to send me to Siberia if I didn't, but it wasn't necessary. Instead, as soon as our conversation ended, I headed to the closet and dug out my skates. And as I slipped them on right there in the living room, I suddenly began to wonder if maybe, just maybe, somewhere out there the Cleveland Barons' own Len Frig was doing the exact same thing.

4

New Jerseys

I started playing organized hockey when I was eleven. It seemed unfathomably old to me at the time, since I'd read that Gretzky pretty much skated out of the womb.

"I've got a lot of catching up to do if I ever hope to make it to the pros," I thought.

The bigger issue, of course, was that up until that point, I had never really demonstrated much of anything one might confuse with natural athletic ability—my football career, for example, was highlighted by accidentally running into a tree.

But if there's anything I've learned in this life, it's that a little misguided confidence never hurt anyone. And with that in mind,

I asked my dad to let me try out for the travel team shortly after he signed me up to play in the Cleveland Heights peewee hockey league, even though I technically had yet to set foot on the ice for an actual game of hockey as a member of anything even slightly resembling a team. In short, I "sucked," to the use the parlance of my youth—and also now. But I sure as hell wasn't going to let that stop me.

"These coaches have been around," I thought. "Surely they'll appreciate the opportunity to work with someone unfettered by any preconceived notions of the game or how it might be played and immediately set about molding me into a hockey great."

I was insane, but whatever.

The travel team, of course, was made up of boys who could skate circles around all the other eleven-year-olds in town and, as such, would play against all the other boys within a hundred miles or so who also did not suck at hockey in the least. Darwinism being what it is, most of the kids on the travel team were more physically developed than their peers and, adding insult to injury, were better-looking, too. They had cool names like Trip and Badger. And some even had totally sweet hockey hair at an age when most other kids were still settling for prepubescent bowl cuts doled out by local barbers who knew nothing about how games were won.

But the best thing about the travel team was their jerseys. They were black and gold, the official colors of Cleveland Heights, and the same colors worn by the city's powerhouse high school hockey team. On the chest was the official Cleveland Heights logo, the letters *CH* in the shape of a tree with leaves

sprouting off the letters and everything. It wasn't exactly menacing, but still, to wear this jersey gave one instant credibility
around town as someone who was among the very best in the
area at hockey, at least as far as eleven-year-olds go. The travel
team players even had a special patch sewn on their satin hockey
jackets that alerted everyone to their hockey awesomeness even
when they were nowhere near a rink.

You may have seen this coming, but no matter how badly I
wanted to wear that black and gold jersey and the cool jacket
that went with it, I didn't make the travel team that year. Or the
year after that. By the third year, I was a hardened thirteen-year-
old and skipped tryouts altogether, rationalizing to myself that
it was a "rebuilding year" for me anyway.

Not making the travel team, of course, meant being assigned
to one of the three house league teams, which were made up of
everyone from kids who were good but not quite good enough
to play for the travel team on down to wide-eyed beginners in
spotless new equipment who could barely stand on the ice without desperately clinging to the boards. But what united us house
league players was the fact that we'd be wearing jerseys that
were anything but black and gold. Some were green and yellow,
others were blue and white, but regardless of their colors, they
all sent a quiet message—at least to me and, presumably, all
those cool kids who made the travel team—that we were average, at best, at hockey.

Looking back on it, most of the above reads to me as early
warning signs of a disturbing psychological profile that would
reveal itself in the years that followed. Still, my reverence for the

hockey jersey remains. After all, despite the endless list of factors that can contribute to the success of a hockey team—goaltending, coaching, whether or not the T-shirt cannon guy is allowed to ride the Zamboni—does any of it really matter in the end if the team doesn't also have a seriously awesome jersey?

The answer, of course, is no. And I've got a closet full of hockey jerseys purchased solely on the basis of whether they are awesome or not to prove it.

I realize it is at this point that you might be thinking that hockey jersey appreciation is entirely subjective, and therefore no one person can say definitively whether a jersey is truly awesome or not, thus rendering this entire discussion moot. And to that, I say you are wrong—I am that one person, which is why I have taken the time to analyze this subject very closely and with a precision rarely seen outside of ninja circles. Also, I realize, of course, that a hockey jersey is traditionally called a "sweater" by us purists; I refer to it as a jersey throughout this book so as not to confuse the average reader, who might be enjoying this book not specifically as a book about hockey, but merely as a timeless literary classic to be enjoyed again and again, preferably next to a roaring fire or some other sort of open flame.

Anyway, my first stop when addressing the important subject of hockey jerseys was to speak with my friend Brian Slagel, founder and president of Metal Blade Records. Brian is the guy who gave a little band called Metallica their very first exposure by putting them on a heavy metal compilation back in 1982, before they'd even played a gig. But perhaps more impressive—at least as far as this book is concerned, anyway—is that Brian has what I can only assume is one of the biggest collections of hockey jerseys in the world.

"I had about 2,500 jerseys at one point," Brian told me, "but I gave away about 750 of them to be sold for charity."

I thought to feign disappointment that Brian's jersey collection was now down to a paltry 1,750 or so, but since I have just forty or so in my collection, I just kept things moving and asked if he actually wore all those jerseys.

"I used to wear them all the time," Brian explained. "But now everybody's wearing them, so I don't wear them anymore."

If there's a bigger power move out there than owning 1,750 hockey jerseys—enough that Brian recently decided to buy a second home to house all of them, along with his other hockey memorabilia—and then decidedly *not* wearing any of those jerseys, I have yet to hear about it. But what matters is that Brian and I both really love hockey jerseys. And since I'm the one writing this book, I've taken it upon myself to give what I believe to be the definitive commentary on the current state of jerseys in the game—and, hopefully while I'm at it, figure out if there is any correlation between the quality of hockey jerseys and the popularity of the sport in that particular area.

This probably won't help me get speaking engagements at any NHL banquets (though please know that I intend to show up at several on the back of this book, whether invited or not), but I should probably say right out of the gate that NHL jerseys are generally not as cool as the jerseys in pretty much every other league, and everyone knows it. The reason for this, I'm guessing, is that NHL jerseys are designed to appeal to the masses—grown men, small children, nuns, even the occasional urologist—and, as a result, play it a little too safe and nonviolent-looking for my tastes, which is why I tend to look to minor league, junior and European teams for true hockey jersey greatness.

One of the very best hockey jerseys, in my expert opinion, belongs to the Sudbury Wolves of the Ontario Hockey League, where hockey legend Ron Duguay played before he and his incredible hair turned pro. Sudbury's jersey is mostly blue (a strong color, generally speaking) and features a completely deranged-looking wolf on the chest with fresh blood on its teeth. What really takes things to the next level, though, is that the wolf also has droplets of blood actually flying off the teeth, a detail that suggests that the wolf has not only just killed something, but he may very well still be in the process of dismembering it, which is awesome. Add to that the fact that the whole thing looks like it was drawn by a fifteen-year-old hopped up on Mountain Dew and you have a jersey that all but guarantees victory for the Wolves each and every time they hit the ice.

"But Dave," you say, "the Sudbury Wolves have never even won an Ontario Hockey League championship."

And to that I say, "Whatever—it's definitely not the jersey's fault. The important thing is that Sudbury has an amazing jersey and the sport is wildly popular in the area, so you tell me."

The Jacksonville Icemen of the ECHL is another favorite jersey of mine. This one features some guy who seems really upset about how cold it is outside, even though he presumably lives in Florida and is wearing a winter coat like some drifter hanging out in front of the bus station. I honestly have no idea what's going on with this guy—he seems complicated and not exactly crazy about the cards he's been dealt in life, but more importantly he looks like he wants to kill someone, which is great if you want to win games. I should probably also mention that the guy in question is holding a hockey stick, which really drives home the point that this is a hockey jersey.

The Quebec Major Junior Hockey League's Baie-Comeau Drakkar have a jersey so amazing, it's almost two jerseys in one, as far as I'm concerned. This one features a Viking ship with an unhinged and—if I'm being honest—slightly high-looking dragon on the bow. This honestly would have been enough to ensure jersey greatness on its own. But then, upon closer inspection, you can see the heads of a bunch of Vikings sticking out of the boat while they row straight on through an iceberg using hockey sticks instead of oars, even though that definitely makes it a million times harder. You can just tell that when the Vikings finally decide to get out of that boat, anyone they come across is pretty much screwed. I have no idea what the Baie-Comeau Drakkar's record was last season, but I can only assume it was amazing.

Meanwhile, over in Russia, you have the Kontinental Hockey League's Traktor Chelyabinsk, whose amazing jersey—up until recently, at least—featured an enraged polar bear actually biting a hockey stick in two! How is he supposed to play the game with a broken stick? Yeah, right—like he even cares. I'll tell you this much: you see a Traktor opponent coming at you with this nutjob of a polar bear on his chest, and you'll think twice about even trying to play the puck.

Despite my preference for non-NHL jerseys, the NHL has its fair share of solid jerseys, too. And while I had originally intended to rate and review each and every one of them in this chapter, I don't want to offend anyone by saying how, for example, I think the Tampa Bay Lightning's logo looks more like something a car alarm company might have embroidered onto golf shirts for their annual team-building seminar than the logo of a hockey team looking to win games. And before you try to remind me how Tampa Bay has already won three Stanley Cups, including consecutive ones in 2020 and '21, I ask you to simply consider how many more they could have won by now had they had a better jersey. See, Tampa Bay? I'm here to help, not hurt.

With that in mind, here are just a few helpful, take-'em-or-leave-'em suggestions on how each NHL team could improve its jersey and, in the process, perhaps even start winning way more games without even really trying. And more importantly, I am certain that if the NHL had even slightly cooler jerseys, the popularity of hockey in the United States would skyrocket. With that in mind, if anyone from any of these organizations happens to be reading this and would like to incorporate some of my ideas into your new-and-improved jersey for next season, please know you may have these ideas entirely free of charge. I present them simply out of a love for the game and not because I am hoping to get free nachos or anything, even though that would rule and actually seems like a relatively easy way to thank me, all things considered.

Anaheim Ducks

Anaheim's jersey has the footprint of a duck on the chest. Who is afraid of that? No one. Not even other ducks. What Anaheim might consider is the fact that a duck penis is not only cork-screwed, but also has backward-pointing spikes on it. Put that on your jersey instead, Anaheim, and I guarantee your opponents will eventually just stop showing up for games altogether—which, of course, spells instant victory for you guys. This jersey would also give everyone a chance to really learn something, which is honestly the main reason I got into writing books in the first place.

Arizona Coyotes

The Coyotes' original jersey features a coyote that arguably looks pretty cool, but at the same time looks like he's just kind of sad because he can't find his friends. More recently, Arizona introduced a second jersey with a logo that looks like what Picasso might have come up with if he were opening a Tex-Mex restaurant in a strip mall outside of Tucson. And as much as I would totally like to eat at that restaurant the more I think about it, I've encountered plenty of actual coyotes over the years, and as best I can tell, when they're not just standing there trying to creep you out in a 7-Eleven parking lot in Bakersfield, California, or something, they're straight up mur-dering your pets. Put either one of those scenarios on your jersey, Arizona, and I promise you the Stanley Cup is yours for the taking.

Boston Bruins

The Bruins' jersey, like that of most Original Six teams, is a timeless classic that makes me think of a simpler time when Phil Esposito and Bobby Orr were skating around without helmets while being awesome at hockey. And while I don't necessarily even think they need to change it, I'd still love to see a Bruins jersey with an angry bear on it that looks like it's about to maim an entire summer camp just outside Wellesley, Massachusetts. You have the angry bear in the background, and then a bunch of terrified children and camp counselors running for their lives in the foreground. It's a simple, clean design that will no doubt help put the Bruins back on top.

Buffalo Sabres

One could argue that the Sabres' logo, consisting of a buffalo with some sabres beneath it, is a little on the nose, but it's still one of my all-time favorites of the league. In fact, I almost don't want to suggest any changes here, either. Then again, if Buffalo ever decided to ditch their classic logo in favor of a jersey that featured legendary Sabres center Gilbert Perreault devouring a dozen wings on the front, and then maybe a tub of ranch or blue cheese dressing on each shoulder, I would be the first in line to buy all of them, basically.

Calgary Flames

The Calgary Flames' logo, just like that of the Atlanta Flames before them, is simple and to the point—it's a letter *C* and it's on fire. What more do you want? Add to that the fact that when the

Flames score goals during home games, the scoreboard shoots out flames so hot, I practically lost my eyebrows at the Saddledome a few years back, and you have hands down one of the best jerseys in the history of the game. It's also worth noting that Canada's answer to the Bloody Mary, the vastly superior Bloody Caesar, was invented in Calgary, and the more of them you drink, the better the Flames jersey starts to look—and you just want to start hugging people. With that in mind, if I were to suggest an alternative jersey for Calgary, it would be one that features me with singed eyebrows and a Bloody Caesar in each hand trying to embrace a guy in a cowboy hat without his consent. Then again, as I understand it, the terms of our settlement would absolutely forbid this sort of thing.

Minnesota Wild

The Minnesota Wild's jerseys get off to a great start with a winning combination of forest green, red, gold and a fourth color I'm told is called "Minnesota wheat," but which we all know is just tan (get over yourselves, Minnesota!). It gives the jerseys a sort of woodsy feel, which is great because it suggests that someone may very well be murdered in the woods at some point, and I have stared at this jersey long enough to know. But the Wild's logo, with its tastefully rendered animal of indeterminate origin (Is it a bear? A cat? A third animal that is the result of an improbable tryst between a bear and a cat? The debate rages on.), looks more like a logo for a bed and breakfast just outside Edina than one for a professional hockey team. Just a friendly suggestion, but why not put the original lineup of the

Replacements* on the chest instead? I promise you they were much wilder than whatever that thing is on your jersey now.

Edmonton Oilers

Edmonton's current predominantly orange home jerseys are nauseating at first glance, but that's part of the genius—you see the Oilers coming at you in these jerseys and you immediately want to look away, or maybe even just head back to the airport altogether, something that can only give them the edge over opponents. Also, the Oilers' logo is simple and to the point—their name is the Oilers, so it says OILERS, and then there is a big drop of oil. Whoever came up with it probably finished before lunch and rightly took the rest of the day off. I'm not saying the Oilers should definitely go back to the predominantly blue jerseys of the Gretzky era and also change their logo to a big oil shaft that spurts blood instead of oil, but I'm fairly confident that any Edmonton fans reading this sentence right now will eventually demand it.

Los Angeles Kings

The Kings' original purple and gold jerseys were amazing. When Gretzky came to town in 1988, however, LA not only switched the team colors to black and silver, but also seemed to begin an active campaign of making their jersey less and less awesome with each passing season. If I played for the

---

* I shouldn't have to explain this, but the Replacements, along with fellow Twin Cities legends Hüsker Dü, were one of the greatest rock bands of all time.

Kings—and I've considered it—I would refuse to leave the locker room until they brought back those sweet purple and gold jerseys they had back when Marcel Dionne was showing everybody what's what. In fact, I might even be doing that right now, and you wouldn't even know it.

San Jose Sharks

The San Jose Sharks were founded during the teal sports jersey boom of the early nineties, and thirty years later they still somehow haven't gotten around to getting better team colors (unless, of course, you like the color teal, in which case these jerseys are very nice). Also, their logo is an angry shark devouring a hockey stick instead of, say, an entire human family from Encinitas, so it all feels like one big missed opportunity to me. What I'd really like to see, though, is for San Jose to have a jersey with the mother who slaps Chief Brody after the shark eats her kid in the movie *Jaws*. I honestly think that could even look good on teal.

Vancouver Canucks

I really like the Canucks' current blue jerseys, but if they ever decided to go back to the "Flying V" jersey they had in the seventies and eighties, you'd get no complaints from me. Sure, a lot of people hated those jerseys, but I thought they made the team look cool and also weirdly German at the same time. As an added bonus, if you wear this jersey around the house, you look like a character from a lost *Star Trek* episode—another win, if you ask me. Then again, if Vancouver made an all-new jersey that just has some guy flipping the bird to a map of Toronto, I bet that would look pretty cool, too. This is a reference, of course, to the ongoing rivalry between the two cities that transcends hockey and can even include people who are just out shopping and stuff. Don't mind me—I'm just a guy who totally gets how Canadian intercity relationships work.

Vegas Golden Knights

The Golden Knights' jerseys have a great color scheme, but why they went with just a knight's helmet for their logo instead of a full-on knight smacking an enemy knight directly in the head with a flail or a mace or something, I'll never know in a million, trillion years. Also, as long as I'm on the topic, calling themselves the Vegas Golden Knights instead of the Las Vegas Golden Knights feels kind of lazy to me. Are you really in that much of a hurry that you can't use the full name of your city in your team name, guys? It's one syllable and three extra letters. We can all make the time. Anyway, aside from that thing about the knight smacking another knight in the head, I suggest no changes here, "Vegas."

Carolina Hurricanes

Carolina's jerseys start off great by having red as one of the main colors, because that's the same color as blood. But I've been staring at their logo for the past forty-five minutes straight, and I still have no idea what it's supposed be. Also, their name is the Hurricanes—the least they could have done is have a few squiggly lines somewhere on the jersey to suggest a brisk wind.

Alternatively, they could maybe add some guy loading up all of his possessions into the back of a pickup truck before he heads to Akron to stay with extended family until the whole thing literally blows over. That's a horrible idea that I just came up with while dehydrated, but I swear it's still fifty times better than the current Hurricanes jersey.

Columbus Blue Jackets

With its patriotic red, white and blue color scheme and star logo, Columbus Blue Jackets' jerseys would be great if they were for a beer league team sponsored by a local bank or something. In fact, if I were looking to open a savings account, I would have no problem giving my money to the Columbus Blue Jackets. But last I checked, the Blue Jackets were named after Ohio's Union infantry from the Civil War. Keeping that in mind, why not put Jefferson Davis or Robert E. Lee impaled on a hockey stick on the jersey instead? If they did this, I'd be the first in line for season tickets, and I don't live anywhere near Columbus.

New Jersey Devils

Your name is the Devils and you don't put the full image of Satan—or at least an evil goat on your jersey—instead of merely hinting at evil by putting a devil tail and some horns on the letter *J*? I give up, New Jersey. Call me when you're ready to play hockey. That said, as far as not-nearly-satanic-enough-for-my-tastes jerseys go, the Devils' jersey is fine. I'll also admit to getting a big kick out of their alternate jersey, which just says JERSEY on it. Whoever thought of this deserves a big fat raise.

New York Islanders

Even though the Islanders' logo is just a map of Long Island with a stick and puck thrown in for good measure, their jerseys are still some of the coolest in the league, and they've got the Stanley Cup wins to prove it. That said, I'd still like to see an alternate jersey featuring Big Edie and Little Edie from *Grey Gardens* on the chest. And if that's somehow too niche for the game or even this book, maybe go with a guy in a tracksuit holding a vape pen while shotgunning a can of White Claw in the Smith Haven Mall parking lot instead.

Philadelphia Flyers

I still have no idea what a "Flyer" is and would even go as far as to argue that it's spelled wrong. That having been said, Philadelphia's jerseys are pretty great, and the fact that they haven't changed much at all since the Broad Street Bullies era gives the jersey a nice, violent look just by association, which is great. I still think their mascot, Gritty, might have a dark past that could come back to haunt him one day, but we don't need to get into that right now. As for an alternative jersey suggestion, I'd love to see something with a guy asking for a glass of "wooder," but that honestly sounds like a design nightmare the more I think about it.

Pittsburgh Penguins

Since I grew up in Cleveland, and have thus witnessed countless matchups between the Cleveland Browns and Pittsburgh Steelers whether I wanted to or not, I've been conditioned to believe any team sporting black and gold jerseys is probably going to win.* All to say, the Penguins' jerseys have already got that going for them. Add to the mix a cool hockey-playing penguin that somehow appears both angry and child-friendly at the same time, and it's no wonder the Penguins have won five Stanley Cups. Does it seem weird that a penguin, whose natural habitat is frequently covered in ice, would need ice skates to get around? Maybe. Other than that, I don't really have many improvements to suggest, other than to maybe add blood to the penguin as if it has just attacked something, sort of like the wolf on the Sudbury jersey I was talking about earlier. In fact, this is a note that could apply to every jersey mentioned in this chapter.

Washington Capitals

Despite the fact that the Capitals' jerseys feature maybe the most basic logo of the entire NHL—it's just words, mostly—they still look pretty cool as long as you don't spring for really good seats, at which point you realize that thing I was just saying about their logo. Personally, I would rather see them with a jersey that depicts a family of four from Indianapolis visiting DC for the first time to check out all the monuments and maybe hit some of the shops, but I'm honestly starting to wonder whether I even deserve a job with the Capitals organization in the first place at this point.

---

* Calm down, fellow Clevelanders. I just looked it up and, as of this writing, Pittsburgh leads the all-time series 80–62–1, so it's not like I'm wrong. I'm not saying I'm happy about it. I'm just stating facts. Now, go Browns!

Detroit Red Wings

Gordie Howe played for the Red Wings, therefore their jerseys are completely incredible by default. Would their logo work equally well for one of those drive-through auto lube places my friends and I used to make immature but still really funny jokes about back in high school? Of course. But I'm not even sure why you're bringing that up. That said, if Detroit wanted to make jerseys with local rap duo Insane Clown Posse on the chest instead, I bet it would really confuse opponents. In fact, I just checked Insane Clown Posse's website after writing that last sentence, and it turns out they're already selling the exact same jersey I just described. It feels great to be so right about something.

Florida Panthers

The Panthers' current jersey looks pretty cool, but if I'm being completely honest, the panther depicted on the chest looks like it's trying to think of the best life insurance policy for you and your loved ones—God forbid anything should happen to you, like you get attacked by a panther, for example—rather than winning hockey games. To that end, why not keep that same panther, but just have it attacking a shirtless guy in jean shorts who was on his way to the gas station to grab a pack of Marlboros and one of those Monster energy drinks? It doesn't have to be that exact guy, but think of the branding opportunities, Florida!

Montreal Canadiens

Even if I weren't actively trying to avoid getting murdered by an angry mob of Quebecois, I would tell you that the Canadiens have one of the best, if not *the* best, jerseys in the league. In fact, the Habs' jersey is so great that if an angry mob of Quebecois indeed decided to pummel me while wearing Canadiens jerseys, I'd probably mostly remember it as the time I met all those people wearing the cool jersey. That said, it has come to my attention that some people think the Canadiens' logo looks like a toilet seat. And while I think anyone who says that is pretty much nuts, I will also take this as an opportunity to suggest an alternate Canadiens jersey that features a steaming plate of poutine on the chest, and then a Fairmount bagel on one shoulder and a St-Viateur bagel on the other. Crazy, maybe, but still better than the toilet seat some people claim to be seeing here.

Ottawa Senators

The original Senators' logo looked like some girl's boyfriend who begrudgingly agreed to go to a costume party with her in hopes of salvaging their relationship after what happened in Cancún. But that was still better than their current logo, which looks like the same guy, only now he's given up on relationships altogether. A simple solution would be to have a centurion driving a spear right through some ancient Greek guy's head on the front of the jersey, but only if the Senators feel like winning the Stanley Cup. Could someone with a firmer grasp of ancient history improve upon this idea? Definitely, which is why I've asked my publisher to set up a dedicated phone line to take your suggestions today, all you ancient history buffs.

Tampa Bay Lightning

In case I haven't mentioned it already, with the exception of the Los Angeles Kings, I have a natural bias against NHL teams in cities where snow and ice don't naturally and regularly occur,* so Tampa Bay is off to a bad start with me already. That said, I already feel kind of bad about what I said about their jersey earlier in this chapter. I also realize the likelihood of a car alarm company going to the trouble of having a team-building semi-nar isn't great, so my comments were an overreach on so many levels, and it's probably time I take a good, hard look in the mirror. I'd just like to see what Tampa Bay might come up with for a jersey if they spent even fifteen minutes longer brainstorm-ing instead of just saying, "Hey, let's just throw a lightning bolt that looks like we got it from a free clip art catalog on the front and call it a day." Okay, I'm sorry—I'm being mean again. Let's just move on to the next jersey while the entire city of Tampa and I take some time to heal together.

Toronto Maple Leafs

As previously mentioned, I have a soft spot for any Original Six jersey. And as much as most of my jersey improvement sugges-tions tend to encourage violence, I fully admit it would be weird and possibly even anti-science to have a violent leaf on the

---

* Please note that, while definitely feeling this way, I will acknowledge that having professional teams in warmer climates is key to the growth of the sport on its path to becoming the most popular sport in the United States, so I will ultimately allow it.

jersey, so it feels wrong to suggest that right now. Then again, now that I've just said it, I would actually like to see what that might look like. Chlorophyll everywhere, I'm guessing.

Chicago Blackhawks

Rather than wade into the debate over whether it's time the Blackhawks change both their name and jersey for obvious reasons, I'd like to suggest that if Chicago just went ahead and renamed their team after the city's iconic—and undrinkable, according to some people—bäsk liquor, Jeppson's Malört, and then just had a giant bottle of Malört as their logo, they would pretty much have the greatest jersey in the history of sports. And the fact that I am giving these ideas away for free is absolutely killing me right now.

Dallas Stars

The Dallas Stars' jerseys are solid, but they will never be as cool the jersey for the Minnesota North Stars, the team from whence they came, which is why I suggest they make a fresh start for themselves and instead have a jersey that interprets the team's name literally and features the entire cast of the hit TV show *Dallas* on the chest. In fact, now that I'm picturing it, you put Larry Hagman in the foreground and everyone else scattered around behind him based on overall likability. And if there is a more amazing idea for a hockey jersey out there today, I'm all ears.

Nashville Predators

You probably saw this coming, but with the addition of just a little (or preferably a lot) of blood, the Nashville Predators could have a truly stellar jersey. Still, last time I checked, they've yet to bring home a single Stanley Cup, so maybe it's time for a fresh start. Keeping that in mind, what if they ditched the sabre-toothed cat altogether and replaced it with some creepy-looking guy hanging out the driver's seat window of an old cargo van while waving around a handful of candy just down the block from the Grand Ole Opry? Controversial? Maybe. But you don't win games by playing it safe!

St. Louis Blues

Make no mistake, I love the St. Louis Blues' jerseys almost as much as I hate the Tampa Bay Lightning's jerseys. That said, if you really want to drum up a bit more team spirit, instead of the "blue note," why not go with something more frenzy-inducing and put St. Louis's favorite son, the great poet, playwright, literary critic and editor T.S. Eliot, on the jersey instead? It's been suggested by some in the past that I'm not an everyman, but I'm pretty sure this idea proves the naysayers wrong once and for all. This jersey will be big with kids, and also everybody, and I can't even believe I just thought of it.

Winnipeg Jets

The Jets' current jerseys are decent, but anyone who says they are anywhere near as good as the jerseys the old, similarly named but totally different Winnipeg Jets wore before them should be locked up. But rather than starting an argument, may I suggest an alternate jersey featuring Winnipeg's own Randy Bachman, from Bachman-Turner Overdrive, ripping the solo to "Takin'

Care of Business" as the logo, something I mention not only because I think it would really turn heads but also because I would really love to own that jersey.

Seattle Kraken

As I sit here typing this, the Seattle Kraken, the newest addition to an already crowded league, have played just two full seasons, so I'll go easy on them and say I've seen the jerseys the team will be wearing for their inaugural season and I really love the color combination. That said, when the Kraken are ready to take being in the NHL seriously, they might consider that their namesake is an awesome and gigantic sea monster from Scandinavian folklore, and maybe, just maybe, you put *that* on the jersey instead of just some letter *S* that looks incapable of killing anything really, much less an entire ship full of Swedish fishermen immune to joy, pain and everything in between after endless months at sea. Then again, maybe Seattle doesn't want to win hockey games.

New York Rangers

My love for the Original Six aside, as a New York City resident I'm understandably partial to the Rangers and their jersey. That said, it's hard to look at it without also imagining some guy from Bay Ridge wearing dad jeans and a fanny pack while passed out on Eighth Avenue after a particularly thirsty game at the Garden. Keeping that in mind, what if they kept everything the same as their current jersey, but then, instead of just having their name down the front, have the logo be the guy I just described instead?

After all, what is a team without its fans? Hmmm—pretty sure I smell another Stanley Cup at last.

Colorado Avalanche

The Avalanche's jersey is one of the best in the league. Then again, if they would have just used the old and also amazing Colorado Rockies' jersey, and maybe added some poor schmuck trapped under a bunch of snow to the bottom of the logo instead, they probably would have won even more Stanley Cups by now. Better yet, if they had just kept the jerseys from the Quebec Nordiques, the team they originated from, and added the guy trapped under snow I just told you about, they would pretty much never not win games, I bet. I can't believe how good I am at this.

•••

I'm mildly concerned at this point that I may very well have offended fans of virtually every NHL team with this arguably overly in-depth jersey analysis, so let's get back to that house league hockey team I used to play for. The good news is that after three seasons, and despite never making the travel team, I still managed to make my high school's varsity hockey team the following year. And never mind that St. Ignatius's varsity hockey team at the time was awful. What mattered was that I was finally wearing the right jersey—the official blue and gold jersey of the St. Ignatius Wildcats. And for the first time in my short hockey career, I felt something resembling complete. And yes, the jersey also came with a varsity letterman jacket I could wear around school in an effort to project an air of hockey superiority over the other 1,500 or so kids in school, even though most of them probably never had any interest in the sport whatsoever. As I write this, I'm reminded that my niece found that jersey and jacket in my parents' basement some years back and took them home with her. And if she's reading this right now, I want her to know I'd like them back.

5

The Greatest Hockey Team in Kenya

Given my affinity for awesome hockey jerseys, I was on the internet recently, searching that very topic, when I happened upon a striking kelly-green jersey with black and red stripes and a big heraldic lion holding a hockey stick in its mighty paws on the chest. The jersey was for a team called the Kenya Ice Lions, and I wanted one immediately. I also assumed Kenya, in this case, must be referring to some small town in Canada I'd never heard of, and definitely not the arguably more popular country in East Africa. But upon further reading, I learned that the Kenya Ice Lions were indeed located in the country of Kenya—Nairobi, to be exact—and not the small Canadian town it turns out exists only in my mind.

I also learned that not only were the Ice Lions the only ice hockey team in all of Kenya, but they also skated on the only ice rink in the entire country, located inside Nairobi's Panari Hotel. It turned out I was a bit late to the party, too, as the Ice Lions' story had already spread far and wide among hockey fans a few years back, thanks to a short film about them made by Tim Hortons, the popular Canadian donut concern, in which the team traveled to Toronto for a scrimmage against a team of firefighters who had their work cut out for them after NHL stars Sidney Crosby and Nathan MacKinnon suited up for the Ice Lions as surprise ringers. Last but not least, it turned out my new friend Slava Fetisov had already managed to make it all the way to Kenya to skate with the team. And when I heard this last bit of information, I decided it would be totally weird if I didn't do the same.

Through a bit of Facebook stalking, I was able to track down an Ice Lions player named Ali Kilanga and dropped him a line.

"I would like come to Nairobi and play hockey with you guys," I told him, cutting right to the chase.

Much to my delight, Ali told me to come on over. The only problem, it turned out, is that the team's ice rink had temporarily closed during the pandemic and the players were currently staying in shape by playing roller hockey.

"Not a problem," I told him, neglecting to consider that, despite years of ice hockey experience, I'd never once played roller hockey.

"I think I've got some old Rollerblades in the closet," I thought. "How hard could it possibly be?"

...

I'd never been to Kenya before and, after a bit of googling, learned that the medical community was recommending what seemed like several gallons' worth of injections—some for diseases I'd never even heard of and at least a couple that I'd always wanted to try—prior to making the trip. I assumed these shots might be necessary were I to be hanging out on a savanna in a pith helmet and goggles while intermittently submerging myself in whatever standing water might be available, and perhaps not entirely crucial for an intercontinental hockey mission. Still, just looking to get out of the house, I made a doctor's appointment for the first time in roughly fifteen years anyway, at which I unfortunately learned I had apparently shrunk an inch in height.

"Fear not, Dave," I thought, trying to console myself, "hockey skates always give you three and a half more inches."

More importantly, however, my doctor gave me the roughly forty-seven shots I apparently required to visit Kenya, and I was on my way.

I managed to find a direct flight to Nairobi from New York City and boarded a plane at JFK with what appeared to be mostly Kenyans and older Americans who, based on their loose-fitting clothing, animated discussions on wildlife and complete disregard for hair care, looked like they might be going on a bucket list vacation of some sort. Either way, I was confident I was the only one retrieving hockey equipment at baggage claim once we landed after our thirteen-hour flight, and I was feeling pretty self-righteous about it by the time I stepped out of the airport and into the balmy Kenyan air.

"Is this your first time to Kenya?" my cab driver asked as we headed for the city a few minutes later.

"Yes," I told him. "I'm here to play hockey."

"Hockey?" he asked.

"Yes," I replied, "hockey."

"Hockey?"

"Yes, hockey."

We rode in silence for about forty minutes after that, but I could tell he was impressed.

Given that most of my knowledge of Kenya up until this point had been gleaned from nature shows and a quick perusal of the country's Wikipedia page while waiting to get through customs, I assumed I'd see countless lions, tigers and other beasts on the way into town. Who knows? Maybe they'd even walk right up to the car to pop their head in and we'd form lasting friendships people would talk about on the internet for years to come. In the end, though, it was mostly just a lot of cars and motorcycles, the odd bit of roadside construction, and one impossibly lonely-looking man sitting on the side of the road, selling already tied neckties, as if he were hoping to entice commuters into stepping up their look at the last minute.

"Pull over immediately!" I thought to ask my cab driver in an attempt at sounding like I really get how things work around here. "I need a necktie posthaste!"

But I figured he already thought I was a weirdo after I tried to sit in the front seat with him, so I decided against it.

We arrived in Nairobi proper a short while later. Normally, when I travel, I like to stay somewhere more residential in hopes that it might give me a better sense of how the locals live. But since I knew I'd be carrying hockey equipment around, I booked a room at the Stanley Hotel, located in the city's Central Business District, just a few blocks from the parking lot cum roller hockey rink where I assumed I would be completely dominating the Kenya Ice Lions in a few short days.

When my cab pulled up to the hotel, a security guard had a look underneath with a mirror attached to a pole.

"They are making sure we don't have bombs," my driver explained.

I would soon learn this was standard procedure for all cars stopping at the hotel, but at the time it made me feel dangerous, and I liked it.

After dropping off my things in my room, I decided to go for a stroll around the city and maybe grab a cup of delicious Kenyan coffee—or just "coffee," as I assumed it was known in these parts. Downtown Nairobi reminded me a bit of downtown Los Angeles, or even downtown Cleveland if you blur your eyes just right, only with way more people. In fact, there were people pretty much everywhere, crisscrossing every which way as if a massive festival a few blocks away had just let out only moments ago.

As I made my way down a main drag, I couldn't help but notice a guy in a Vancouver Canucks hoodie walk past me.

"Maybe Nairobi is a hockey town after all," I thought.

As it turned out, I would spot tons of folks in hockey gear over the course of my visit. I figured it might be just

Baader–Meinhof phenomenon kicking in,* but twenty-six-year-old Benja, one of the Kenya Ice Lions players I was soon to meet, told me otherwise.

"People wear hockey gear here all the time," Benja told me. "But they have no idea what it is—they just think it looks cool."

I grabbed a coffee and continued my stroll before remembering I hadn't eaten all day and ducking into a restaurant I'd found nearby after searching for Kenyan food on my phone. I was excited to try the local fare and ordered some fish with rice and beans and a red sauce that was so spicy, I assumed the chef might have been trying to pull a prank on me. But with the help of a bottle of Tusker** lager, the local beer of choice, I hope I managed to at least appear that I was in no pain whatsoever.

My Ice Lions contact, Ali, had agreed to meet up with me the next night, Friday, for what he described as "a polite drink," so I was on my own for the rest of my first day in town. As jet lag kicked in, I decided to head back to the hotel for a nap before plotting my next move.

Normally, on a hockeycentric trip like this, I might search for a game in town, but since the Kenya Ice Lions were literally the

---

* As any of my friends will tell you, the Baader–Meinhof phenomenon is one of my favorite phenomena. In case you don't already know, it is a cognitive bias where, after noticing something for the first time, you start to see it everywhere, like reruns of *The Big Bang Theory*.

** As the story goes, the brewery's founder, George Hurst, was killed in an elephant hunting accident and his brother, Charles, named the beer "Tusker" in his memory. If you ask me, George got what was coming to him for hunting elephants. But I will say it's a delicious beer.

only team in the entire country, I figured I might have to come up with an alternate plan that evening.

The little I'd read about visiting Nairobi suggested it's not a great idea to walk around the city alone at night. But between all those shots I had to get before coming here, the fact that so far I'd been getting nothing but good vibes from this delightful city, and the unmistakable air of menace I try to project whenever in public, I was not to be deterred. I wandered a few blocks, trying and failing to blend in with pedestrian traffic before ducking into a couple bars for a look around. But I was still pretty wiped out from my journey, so in the end I decided to just head back to the hotel for a quiet nightcap while enjoying the beautiful weather at the poolside bar.

My hope, of course, whenever I'm forced to travel alone is that I'll luck into some conversation with a friendly local at a bar or restaurant so that I might get some hot tips on what I might get up to while in town, or maybe even get invited to their home for a quality hang or two. So, I was thrilled when a beautiful young Kenyan woman named Nuru smiled and gestured toward the seat next to her as I approached the hotel bar.

"How are you?" she asked as I settled in.

"Good," I replied. "How are you doing?"

"Good," Nuru smiled before taking a sip of her Coke. "You are visiting Kenya?"

"Yes," I told her. "I'm here to play hockey."

"Sorry?" she asked, sounding weirdly Canadian for a moment.

"Hockey," I repeated. "Ice hockey."

"Ice hockey," she said back to me.

"Yes, ice hockey. Do you know it?"

"Sorry?"

As best I could tell, based on my experience with the cab driver and now this lovely woman at the hotel bar, bringing up hockey was not the path to easy conversation in Kenya. I decided to hit reset and order myself a beer.

"Would you like some company tonight?" Nuru then asked me, bursting the illusion that I'd just happened into some pleasant conversation with a random beautiful woman on my first night in Nairobi.

"Yes, I would," I replied in an attempt at subterfuge. "And you are keeping me wonderful company at this very moment by talking to me at this bar while we sit at a completely respectable distance from each other."

"No, I would like to keep you company in your hotel room," she clarified. "I can give you a massage and then maybe there are other things you might like."

"I like hockey," I told her, doing my best to dazzle her with my naivete. "Is that what you mean?"

"Sorry?" she said once more.

It was at this point that I figured it might be time to finish my beer and call it a night, but as soon as I set my empty bottle down on the bar, a fresh one appeared before me.

"This is from the gentleman at the other end of the bar," the bartender explained.

I assumed my night was about to get even more complicated, but as it turned out, the gentleman in question was just celebrating a birthday and wanted to buy a drink for everyone else at the bar.

"I am Lameck," the fiftysomething birthday boy said, suddenly appearing next to me with an extended hand. "I am from Tanzania."

"Happy birthday, Lameck," I replied, shaking his hand. "Are you interested in a massage by any chance?"

"From you?" he asked guardedly.

"No, from her," I said, pointing to Nuru.

"I already asked him," she snapped. "He's not interested."

"Sorry?" I replied.

"He's not interested," she repeated, seemingly annoyed.

"What brings you to Kenya?" Lameck then asked me.

"Hockey," I told him.

"Hockey?" he replied.

"Yes, hockey," I said again as he slowly backed away toward his seat.

I began drinking my beer more quickly while staring straight ahead in hopes that Nuru might get the hint I was definitely not interested in escalating things in the sex way. It didn't work.

"It will cost one hundred dollars," she suddenly said, picking up our conversation right where it left off.

"American?" I asked, somehow back in it with no resistance whatsoever.

"Yes," she replied.

"I'm sorry," I told her. "The only game I'm here to play is hockey."

"Hockey?

"Yes, hockey! Why does this keep happening every time I say 'hockey' in this town?"

I went back to my beer. And once again, before I could set my empty bottle back down on the bar, another beer appeared before me. I looked down the bar to see birthday boy Lameck smiling and waving at me.

"Thanks for this, but I need to go to bed," I yelled apologetically to him.

"Are you American?" Lameck then asked.

"Yes," I answered.

"If you don't drink that beer, you are a disgrace to your country," Lameck said.

Between my jet lag and the beers already in me, his argument somehow seemed valid, so I started drinking this latest beer while staring straight ahead once more.

"Fifty dollars," Nuru suddenly said.

"Sorry," I said turning to her, "I have a girlfriend."

"So?" she replied. "You should enjoy life."

"I am perfectly satisfied with my current level of life enjoyment," I told her.

Suddenly, Lameck appeared next to me again.

"You know, I trained with American soldiers when I was in the army," he said while standing just a little too close.

"What sort of training?" I asked. "Guns?"

"No," Lameck replied. "If I need a gun to kill you, I will use yours."

"But I don't have a gun," I said.

"That is my point—I don't need a gun to kill you," he continued. "You see what I mean?"

It definitely felt like time to go now, but before I could get up from my seat at the bar, yet another beer appeared in front of me. I reluctantly drank it, if only to somehow honor my country.

"Thirty dollars," Nuru said as I finally stood up to go back to my room a short while later.

"Thirty dollars?" I asked. "Why would you agree to do 'other things I might like' for that price?"

"It's a one-time deal," she replied. "Next time, it's full price."

"There won't be a next time," I told her. "Or a first time!"

I could tell by the look on her face that I had pretty much ruined any chance at friendship with Nuru at this point. But on the plus side, Lameck gave me his phone number and told me to give him a call if I wanted to hang out over the weekend, so, as I drifted off to sleep a short while later, I decided to call my first night in Kenya a draw.

•••

I woke early the next morning and headed out of the hotel in search of breakfast. Along the way, a man offered to shine my running shoes. I politely declined while admiring his can-do attitude. I also spotted a guy in a Toronto Maple Leafs T-shirt, which felt like a good omen despite what I would later learn about Kenyans in hockey gear, before eventually stumbling into a café. There, I ordered something called a "Kenyan breakfast," which consisted of eggs, sweet potatoes and some sort of boiled root that was light pink in color. It was delicious, and I especially liked the idea of eating only traditional Kenyan food during my visit.

"This will give me the strength I need to dominate the Kenya Ice Lions on Sunday," I thought, "even though I have technically never played roller hockey in my life."

After breakfast, I jumped in a cab to somewhere I'd read about called Village Market, where I could supposedly load up on Kenyan trinkets to shower my loved ones with upon my return home from this beautiful country. As we drove past immaculately landscaped embassies and estates on our way out of the city, my driver began to tell me about various places in the area I could go to see wild animals.

"You meet crocodiles, you meet ostriches," he explained. "You can even meet giraffes and lions."

I like that he said I could "meet" the animals, instead of just see. It made it sound more like the animals and I might sit down to lunch and perhaps a bit of delightful conversation. Potential maiming aside, it was the kind of world I wanted to live in.

We arrived at Village Market a few minutes later, where I was disappointed to find tourists as far as the eye can see, as it shatters the illusion that I'm the only one visiting from out of town. Still, I soldiered on, eventually gravitating toward a parking garage where a bunch of vendors were selling various Kenyan trinkets. I had heard that the vendors here could be aggressive, but when a woman in her sixties selling painted wooden giraffes began following me around while saying I "insult her business" after failing to actually buy one, it was more than I could handle on this sunny afternoon, so I quickly made my escape, grateful to be giraffeless.

I returned to Nairobi proper and began wandering the city some more, stopping off for a lunch of fried chicken and rice before being drawn toward the sounds of a live band playing upstairs in a building down the street from the restaurant. I entered a stairwell and climbed a few flights to find a band consisting of drums, keyboards, bass and trumpet backing not one but two preachers alternately singing and speaking sweet nothings to the Lord in both English and Swahili in a makeshift chapel inside what otherwise appeared to be an apartment building.

Since there were only three people in the congregation, it was impossible for me to slip in undetected, so I instead just smiled and waved at everybody before taking a seat myself and doing my best to appear as worked up about things as everyone else. It was unclear whether I was witnessing a church service or merely a band practice in anticipation of an upcoming church service, which is why, after I spotted a Gibson Les Paul sitting quietly on a guitar stand in the corner, I considered asking if I could sit in with them and maybe rip a few solos, as is my wont. But I quickly lost my nerve and instead just prayed I might be at least half as good at roller hockey as I'd been hoping when it came time to play with the Ice Lions on Sunday.

I had made plans to meet Ali a short while later, so after I'd either had enough of the Lord or perhaps the other way around, I headed back outside and immediately happened upon Jeevanjee Gardens, a park in the center of the city where there were two separate groups of about forty men each, huddled together while engaging in what appeared to be a heated debate in Swahili.

"What are they talking about?" I asked a young man seated on a bench nearby.

"Politics—there is an election coming," he explained. "Are you visiting Kenya?"

"Yes," I replied. "I'm here to play hockey with the Kenya Ice Lions."

"Hockey?" the man asked.

"Yes, hockey, with the Kenya Ice Lions," I told him. "Do you know them?"

"No."

"They are the greatest ice hockey team in all of Kenya."

I didn't have the heart to tell him they were also the only ice hockey team in all of Kenya. And since it was about time to meet Ali, I decided to just smile awkwardly at him for slightly too long before heading off.

A few minutes later, I met Ali in front of the Nation Centre, a futuristic building that looks straight out of *The Jetsons* and is home to one of Kenya's main newspapers, the *Nation*. One of the nice things about being a pale Irish guy from Cleveland in Nairobi is that I'm hard to miss, so Ali started waving at me from about fifty yards away as I approached. We exchanged greetings and headed to a nearby café for coffee and samosas.

"So, how did you get into hockey?" I asked him as soon as we sat down.

"Before the internet, I used to learn about a lot of stuff from whatever American magazines we could get over here," Ali told me. "One day I was flipping through an issue of the *Source* and they had a picture of a hockey game and I thought, 'What is this?!'"

I loved the idea that a hip-hop magazine was responsible for turning a kid on the other side of the world on to ice hockey, a simple reminder that the world can be magic if you just pay attention.

At forty-three, Ali is the elder statesmen of the team and a mentor to many of the younger players, especially those on the Kenya Ice Cubs, an offshoot of the Ice Lions made up of teenagers just learning the game. Ali got the chance to finally play hockey himself while working as an employee at the Panari Hotel, where, of course, what is now the Ice Lions' home rink is located.

"Some people started playing pickup hockey games there, guys from Canada and stuff like that," Ali explained. "And the Kenya Ice Lions came a few years later, in 2016."

As I was packing for my trip to Nairobi, it occurred to me that maybe I could just buy a new stick when I got into town rather than dragging one all the way from my apartment in New York City, but Ali quickly set me straight.

"They don't sell hockey equipment here," he laughed. "Everything we have comes from the United States or Canada."

Another big help has been former NHL player Johnny Oduya, who is Swedish born but half Kenyan.

"Johnny has been great to us," Ali explained. "He's given us a bunch of equipment and even custom jerseys."

After finishing up at the café, Ali and I jumped into a cab to go have that "polite drink" he promised me at an open-air bar called the Rabbit Hole a couple miles away, where DJs played old-school hip-hop and R&B at pummeling volumes and a crowd ranging in age from twenties to fifties eased into the weekend.

"We'll have two beers," Ali yelled to our waiter as soon as we grabbed a table.

Our waiter returned a couple minutes later with not two but four bottles of beer and set them down in front of us. As I would soon learn over the course of the evening, and indeed the rest of my visit to Nairobi, ordering "a beer" at a local bar actually means two beers unless you look the waiter in the eye and practically beg him to bring just one beer, not that I'm complaining.

As Ali and I began to bond over drinks and our mutual love of hockey, I decided to ask what he had meant by a "polite drink," as, given my nagging insecurities, I assumed it was a euphemism for "a hopefully brief drink with this nutjob who came here all the way from America just to play hockey."

"You see that table over there?" Ali said, pointing to a couple of men seated next to us with an entire bottle of Johnnie Walker between them. "*That* is the opposite of a polite drink."

I was relieved and even a bit flattered to learn that Ali simply meant that he didn't want me to spend the night puking in the back of a Nairobi cab, as thrilling as that sounds on some level. Still, hoping to land somewhere just shy of that, we moved on from the Rabbit Hole to another open-air bar located farther out of town called Numero 5, owned by Ali's childhood friend Larry.

The crowd at Numero 5 was a bit younger, but the blaring old-school hip-hop and R&B was the same, which was just fine by me, as those are my jams. Ali spotted Larry holding things down at the end of the bar and walked me over to introduce me.

"This is Dave," Ali said to Larry, a burly man in his forties wearing a baseball hat and tracksuit. "He came here from New York to play hockey."

Larry shook my hand and nodded at me with the bemused look that everyone I'd talked to in Nairobi so far—besides Ali—seemed to get on their faces when the word *hockey* was mentioned. As I regarded Larry's confusion, I imagined a time in the hopefully not-too-distant future when, if you told someone you came to Nairobi to play hockey, they'd give you a look that said, "Of course—it would be weird if you came to Nairobi and *didn't* play hockey."

Ali seems to be into that idea, too.

"We're not quite ready to join the International Ice Hockey Federation," he said of the sport's worldwide governing body over another double round of beers, "but we will be soon."

After narrowly dodging a young man relieving himself of the contents of his stomach onto the sidewalk on my way back from the restrooms a short while later, Ali and I figured we'd wrung just about all the fun we could out of the night and grabbed a cab back into town.

We met up the following morning at the hotel and walked to a nearby restaurant for an outdoor breakfast of fish and rice, during which he told me about Tim Hortons bringing the Kenya Ice Lions to play in Toronto in 2018.

"That was awesome," Ali said, beaming.

As it turned out, only twelve of the Kenya Ice Lions—which is, of course, to say two full lines—made the trip, as some of the players on the team lacked passports or even the birth certificates necessary to get a passport in the first place.

"Tim Hortons gave us all brand new equipment when we got there," Ali continued. "And we got a private tour of the Hockey Hall of Fame after it closed."

As someone who has been to the Hockey Hall of Fame at least four times that I can remember, I was a little jealous. Don't even get me started on the fact that Tim Hortons gave gift cards to all the players, thus allowing them to eat complimentary Timbits throughout their visit. The only thing missing to make this the most Canadian experience ever, in my estimation, was if Geddy Lee himself had picked them up at the airport.

"We played hockey for over three hours," Ali continued. "They had to kick us out of the rink!"

As we finished our meal, Ali pointed at a tall building in the distance.

"That's the KICC building," he said. "The man who designed that building said it was inspired by a donkey penis."

I wondered if Ali might be messing with me. But now I'm talking about a donkey penis in this book, so the joke is on him. Or, actually, maybe the joke is still on me, the more I think about it. In any case, the KICC, or Kenyatta International Convention Centre for long, does indeed look like a donkey penis,* at least as far as buildings go, anyway.

"The parking lot where we'll play roller hockey tomorrow is

---

* Actually, I couldn't resist doing a little internet digging and can confirm that one of the building's architects, David Mutiso, has, in fact, stated that he was inspired by a donkey penis when designing the building. Then again, don't most tall buildings look sort of like donkey penises if you really think about it?

not far from the KICC building," Ali told me as soon as I stopped giggling about the whole donkey penis thing.

"You mean the donkey penis building?" I asked.

"Yes, but we don't call it the donkey penis building," Ali corrected me.

"You might not," I told him, "but I will only be referring to it as the donkey penis building moving forward."

If you are growing annoyed at how many times I have used the phrase "donkey penis" in the last few paragraphs, imagine how Ali felt hanging out with me throughout the remainder of my visit, a period of time in which I worked the phrase into conversation so much, you would have sworn I was the world's preeminent equine urologist.

After breakfast, Ali walked me over to the parking lot where we'd be skating the next day.

"All these cars will be gone," he told me. "The whole parking lot is reserved for skating on Sundays."

As he spoke, I surveyed the parking lot while looking forward to completely dominating anyone else on skates who dared to show up the next day. It felt good.

From the parking lot, Ali and I moved on to a souvenir shop, where I purchased my lone tchotchke of the trip: a small elephant head carved out of wood that I was certain would annoy my girlfriend just the right amount when I hung it on our already crowded living room wall upon my return.

My elephant head in hand, I walked with Ali to a small department store, where he picked up some school supplies for a couple of the Kenya Ice Cubs players.

"They have exams coming up," he explained. "We try to help them out any way we can."

From the department store, I followed Ali through the crowded streets of downtown Nairobi, where cars, buses, motorcycles and people moved in all directions, regardless of any street signs or traffic signals, which, as best I could tell, were merely suggestions one can take or leave depending on one's mood and not something anyone strictly follows in Nairobi.

"It's organized chaos," Ali said with a smile as a motorcycle passed in front of us, just narrowly missing our feet. "In a good way!"

Given my penchant for jaywalking and living outside the law in general, I loved it, even if it meant Ali had to save me from getting hit by various vehicles at least a dozen times throughout the day.

With all the people and traffic, downtown Nairobi can already be a bit of a sensory overload, but nothing could have prepared me for what immediately became my favorite thing about Nairobi (and, arguably, Planet Earth as of this writing) as soon as I laid eyes on them: Nairobi's legendary matatus. The matatus are a form of public transportation in the city featuring elaborately decorated vans and buses that usually blast reggae, hip-hop or R&B throughout the trip. Matatu motifs include anything from religious iconography and NBA basketball teams to Colombian drug lord Pablo Escobar and at least one I spotted dedicated entirely to *Soul Plane*, the highly underrated Snoop Dogg theatrical vehicle in which the rapper plays a pilot with a fear of heights and little regard for commercial air travel norms.

When Ali took me to a parking lot full of matatus, I assumed it was just so I could get a closer look at these magnificent contraptions, but when he told me we'd be hopping on one so we could deliver the school supplies he'd just bought, I was downright giddy. And even though the matatu we ended up riding on was a Premier League soccer–themed one that wasn't playing any music onboard for reasons I'll never understand in a million years, I was still thrilled to be going for a spin aboard one.

We rode for about ten minutes before jumping off the matatu in a neighborhood that consisted mostly of small shacks made out of wood or corrugated steel. On the main drag were produce stands, hair salons and assorted tiny convenience stores, most of which had the word *Mamma* in their name.

"That means the owner is mother to a girl named Anna," Ali said of a shop called Mamma Anna that, it's worth noting, had a couple old hockey jerseys for sale.

As Ali and I walked, we passed a man sitting behind a table covered in small piles of bright green leaves.

"Have you ever had khat?" Ali asked me.

"No!" I replied, excited to presumably try a local delicacy. "What's that?"

"It's a bit like cocaine," Ali explained, "except you chew on it."

I figured I was annoying Ali enough with my frequent references to donkey genitalia by this point, so I decided against getting a khat habit started on this particular visit. Still, it was nice to learn something new.

Ali and I moved along before running smack-dab into a motorcycle that had been decorated entirely in decals promoting *The Boss Baby*, the animated film in which Alec Baldwin plays an infant with rare leadership qualities, which just goes to show you can fly to the ends of the earth, but you will never, ever escape Alec Baldwin, no matter how hard you try.

A couple minutes later, after wending our way down an alley through playing children and the occasional stray dog, we entered a small shack that is one of two that are home to Calvin and Brian, two of the Kenya Ice Cub players, and their family, so Ali could drop off the school supplies he had bought for them.

As Ali and Calvin got to chatting about his upcoming exams and tinkering with the wheels on his Rollerblades, I sat near the door as neighborhood kids took turns craning their necks inside the doorway to get a glimpse of the guy from Cleveland.

"Hi, I'm Dave," I'd say with a wave to each of them before they giggled and disappeared, only to be replaced by another curious kid a second later.

"We met a lot of the younger kids after they'd come to watch us play roller hockey," Ali explained on our way back into town on a matatu bus that was blasting reggae, much to my delight. "Then we encouraged them to learn to skate and play hockey— it's a good way to keep them occupied and away from getting involved with gangs, becoming pickpockets and stuff like that."

Ali and I returned to my hotel a short while later, where we were met by Benja.

"He's gonna go with you to your show," Ali told me.

I figured as long as I was coming all this way, I might as well try to get on stage while I was here, so I'd found an

English-language comedy show taking place at a café located in Nairobi National Park that was kind enough to add me to the bill. I'd performed comedy, music or both in about twenty different countries so far, and I saw no reason to spare Kenya as long as I was already there.

On the cab ride out to the show, I was excited to spot the occasional troop of baboons on the side of the road. And I was even more excited to see a couple guys in tribal attire walking along the side of the road as we pulled up to the park.

"Who are they?" I asked Benja.

"They are Maasai warriors," Benja told me.

As I would soon learn, the Maasai are an ethnic group inhabiting parts of Kenya and Tanzania. They dress in brightly colored robes and jewelry and carry cool sticks with them, even though I bet there is another name for those. I wanted to become friends with them immediately.

"This guy Dave seems different from all the other tourists," I imagined the Maasai saying to each other once we had a chance to really get to know each other. "I am so, *so* glad he is hanging out with us."

But before I could become besties with the Maasai people, I had a show to do, so Benja and I continued on to Nairobi National Park.

As we pulled up to the café inside the park where the show was taking place, I noticed there was a family of what I assumed were wild boars milling about. I figure it was at this point that I would be mauled to death, like a scene out of the critically acclaimed eighties television miniseries *The Thorn Birds*. But then

Benja explained that the animals in question were not wild boars, but warthogs, the kinder, gentler cousins to the boar, and that—much to my relief—my odds of being mauled to death weren't very good at all.

Between the warthogs, the Maasai, and the baboons, I was pretty excited by the time Benja and I settled at a table to watch the show until it was my time to perform. Before things started, we got to talking about hockey.

"How long have you been playing?" I asked Benja.

"About two years," he said.

"That's great," I replied while quietly taking comfort in the fact that I had decades of hockey experience over him and would likely be completely dominating him and everyone at the roller hockey game the following afternoon. As I would soon learn, however, doing well at roller hockey wasn't the only thing I was overly confident about on this particular evening.

"Our next comedian is here all the way from New York City," the very funny host for the evening, Ciku Waithaka, said from the stage. "Please welcome Dave Hill."

In my seventeen years of performing comedy, it's only on a handful of occasions that I've said to myself, "This will go well," before hitting the stage. And on every single one of those occasions, I've bombed horribly. But tonight, I was feeling good. I was on the other side of the world just to play hockey, I'd seen baboons just hanging out on the side of the road, and now I was about to do an impromptu comedy set on a delightful Saturday evening in Kenya. So I went ahead and thought, "Yeah, this will go well," as I approached the stage.

And it sure didn't. Fortunately for me, though, I prefer an extreme reaction. So, if the crowd doesn't love me, hate will do just fine. And while I can't say that they definitely hated me, I can confirm that the only big laugh I got on stage that night was after I joked that my set was only going to last "another forty-five minutes or so."

Emboldened by my inaugural, if pitiful, Kenyan comedy performance, Benja and I headed off into the night, where, after stopping so I could get a photo with an armed Kenya Defence Forces solider in which I think both the soldier and I thought we were both going to look much cooler than the photo turned out, we grabbed another cab to a massive open-air nightclub called 1824.

Just like at the other two clubs I'd already been to during my visit, the DJ at 1824 was cranking tunes at skull-vibrating volume and the place was crowded with people of all ages. Since the downstairs area was already packed, a waiter showed us to a table in the upstairs bar overlooking the dance floor, where we were quickly joined at our table by four beautiful young women. I figured these ladies must have gravitated toward us because of the undeniable "We're hockey players" vibe I'd like to think we were giving off, but it turned out they only sat at our table because the seats were the only ones left in the place. Still, that didn't stop Benja and me from having an excellent evening in which we danced, sang and had way too many double rounds of Tusker lager, considering I was supposed to be playing roller hockey for the first time the next day.

I awoke the following morning feeling hungover yet alive,

dammit, for today I would finally be playing hockey in Kenya. In hopes of sweating out the beers from the night before, I went to the hotel gym to run a few miles on the treadmill.

"This way, I'll be totally warmed up when it comes time to destroy the Kenya Ice Lions at roller hockey later today," I thought as I carefully stepped onto the machine. "These clowns won't know what hit 'em."

After a post-workout breakfast near the hotel, I grabbed my hockey equipment and began marching confidently over to the parking lot Ali had shown me the day before. The plan was for me to show up at 2 p.m., when the Kenya Ice Cubs were playing, and meet—while also presumably intimidating—everybody before skating with the Ice Lions at 3 p.m.

As I approached the parking lot, I was surprised to see not just hockey players but at least a few dozen Rollerbladers skating laps around the parking lot as onlookers sat along the stone wall surrounding the park, sipping sodas, eating ice cream, smoking cigarettes or—in at least one instance I managed to witness—all three at once. I spotted Ali with a few kids pulling on their equipment and headed in their direction.

"This is Mama Hockey," Ali said, gesturing toward a forty-something woman in a hijab sitting among all the hockey players as they got ready.

Mama Hockey, as her name hints, helps out with the Kenya Ice Cubs, seeing to it that they get the equipment they need and even making sure the players have been fed. She is also the mother of Hanan, a nineteen-year-old girl who plays for the Ice Lions.

A short while later, Tim Colby, a fiftyish Canadian expat and former minor league hockey coach who started coaching the Ice Lions in 2016, arrived with a pile of new sticks for the players—and, much to my delight, a few Kenya Ice Lions jerseys available for purchase. I snagged one for myself and pulled it on immediately as, had I not spotted it on the internet a couple months earlier, I probably wouldn't be standing in some parking lot in Kenya about to play hockey right now in the first place.

"Are you gonna skate today?" I asked Tim.

"Nah, I don't play roller hockey," he said. "I just stopped by to check in on everybody."

Ali wouldn't be suiting up today, either. Like a few of the other Ice Lions players, he and Tim are purists who save their energy for the ice.

Since I didn't have that option on this particular trip, I threw on my equipment and joined the rest of the Ice Lions on the parking lot "rink" as soon as the Ice Cubs were done playing. For roller hockey, the Ice Lions play three on three with no goalies, instead shooting the puck into tiny street hockey nets no bigger than a microwave. And on the face of things, the players make for a motley crew, as some are suited up in full equipment, complete with face masks, while others wear just skates, gloves and bicycle helmets.

"I should probably go easy on these guys at first," I thought as I rolled toward the center of the parking lot for the opening face-off.

Seconds later, the action was underway and I became instantly aware of how different roller hockey is from ice hockey.

For starters, there's that pesky orange ball used in place of a puck, which bounces all over the place and is much harder to control. Next, I wasn't used to stopping and starting quickly on Rollerblades, which made it hard for me to keep up with the other players or—perhaps more importantly—look even remotely cool as I attempted to play roller hockey for the first time. Add to that the fact that I was roughly twice the age of most of the other players and had been out drinking until 2 a.m. the night before, and it was safe to say I wasn't dominating the Ice Lions nearly as much as I had initially intended when I booked my plane ticket.

"How you doing, Dave?" Trevor, a nineteen-year-old Ice Lion who, despite having only started playing a few months earlier, is already a solid player, asked me.

"I'm g-great," I said while gasping for air.

After about two minutes, I began skating toward the wall where the rest of the Ice Lions players sat waiting to take a shift.

"Who wants to go in for me?" I asked them, collapsing onto the wall.

"You're tired already?" Benja asked me.

"Of course not," I lied. "I just like to take short shifts. You know, like they do in the pros."

Among the hazards of playing roller hockey in a parking lot in Kenya on a Sunday afternoon are, of course, potholes, a large drainage ditch that manages to swallow the ball every few minutes, an ice cream man who has no hang-ups whatsoever about pushing his cart right through the middle of play, and—perhaps most concerning, given that I was finally wearing a brand new

Kenya Ice Lions jersey on my back—what appeared to be hawks* that circled above us almost constantly as we played.

"They like to poop on us," Trevor warned me.

Indeed, most of the area had already been spackled with bird droppings. Still, I wasn't gonna let that stop me from giving it my all out there that day. So, after catching my breath, I headed out for another shift. It didn't go much better, though I did make a mental note to at least try to look like I wasn't about to keel over whenever Ali pointed his camera at me.

As the afternoon wore on, my breaks in between shifts became longer and longer. And I marveled at how skilled the Ice Lions players were at this sport most of them had only started playing a few short years earlier.

"I would love for there to one day be someone from Nairobi playing in the NHL," Ali told me as I sat guzzling water in between shifts.

"Well, I'll do my best to share everything I know about the sport with you guys so that one day that might happen," I told him as I tripped over my own stick and practically fell on my face while trying to stand up a moment later.

I assumed we'd play roller hockey for a couple hours, tops, but the Ice Lions showed no signs whatsoever of slowing down when 5 p.m. rolled around.

---

* I did some polling of a few Ice Lions players, as well as a few random people watching roller hockey, and there was little agreement over what kind of birds these actually were. However, a bit of googling suggests they may have been black kites, a bird of prey commonly found in the city.

"How long do you guys normally play?" I asked Benja, trying to sound more curious than tired.

"Until we can't see the ball anymore," he told me before peeling off on his skates.

I wanted to cry when I heard this. And, were this game taking place near my apartment instead of thousands of miles away on another continent, I would have slowly rolled away without explanation at this point. But since I'd traveled over seven thousand miles to be here, I was determined to go the distance with the Ice Lions on this particular day, so I reluctantly accepted another shift, even though by this point I was mostly just skating big loops around the parking lot while trying to stay upright as the rest of the players managed to actually play the great sport of hockey. Adding insult to injury, at one point a handful of the Ice Cubs joined in the game, so instead of having just guys in their twenties skate circles around me, I was now being humiliated by teenagers, including fifteen-year-old Calvin, who'd seemed like such a nice kid when I'd visited him in his home just the day before, but was now proving to be an absolutely ruthless opponent who openly laughed at me as he skated around me with the ball.

The sun mercifully set sometime around 7 p.m., and I collapsed on a nearby wall to take off my equipment and join the other players in a few rounds of mango juice with mabuyu, a local treat consisting of baobab tree seeds covered in sugar and spices.

"Are you coming back next Sunday?" twenty-one-year-old Gideon, one of the Ice Lions, asked me as I said my goodbyes a short while later.

"Not next Sunday," I told him before slinking off into the night with Benja and Ali in the direction of my hotel. "But I'll be back."

I was exhausted at this point, but Ali said there was a reggae night happening at a club called Taurus a few miles outside town, and I figured if I couldn't get it together to go to a reggae night in Kenya on a Sunday night, then what was I even doing with my life? So, after a quick rinse, I hopped in a cab with them to reggae night.

Along the way, I was surprised to see a handful of fires on the side of the road.

"They're just burning trash," Ali told me.

It's maybe not how I might go about trash disposal, but at the time I kind of liked it, as it gave our drive a fun sort of *Mad Max* vibe.

A short while later, the club appeared on the side of the road, like an oasis in the middle of nowhere. After turning down offers of barbecued intestines from a man standing behind a grill in the parking lot, we headed inside, where the music was absolutely booming—and was so loud, in fact, that conversation was next to impossible. So, Ali, Benja and I just sat back and enjoyed the music over a few beers while Ali passed his phone around to share hockey videos on Instagram. And as the air slowly filled with the kind of scents normally associated with reggae night, I felt as if I might very well be high on hockey after my long day of playing with the Ice Lions.

I woke the following morning impossibly sore but gratefully intact and, after yet another Kenyan breakfast, limped a couple miles to Kenyatta Market, where local women got their hair done and I had a few confusing conversations with shop owners who couldn't make sense of my Cleveland accent.

Later that day, I met up with Ali, and much to my delight, we hopped on another matatu to an area north of the city called Highbridge, where we ate chicken tikka and a fried potato dish called bhaji, washed back with insanely good sugar cane and ginger drinks.

One of my biggest takeaways from the last few days with Ali and the hockey players was that it was as much about community and taking care of each other, especially the younger Ice Cubs, as it was about playing this sport most people don't necessarily think of just yet when they think about Kenya.

"We try to bring them as close to us as we can," Ali says of the Ice Cubs.

As part of the deal, the Ice Cubs have to do their part by staying in school and being good sports in the parking lot on Sundays.

"We won't take away their skates," Ali says of the young players who occasionally fail to hold up their end of the deal. "But we won't give them new wheels."

Of course, I couldn't come all the way to Kenya without at least trying to see a few lions, tigers and other local four-legged types. So, on my last day in Nairobi, I returned to the scene of the crime—aka the abominable comedy set on Saturday night—grabbing a cab back out to Nairobi National Park, where they also offer safaris and have an animal orphanage. The safari turned out to be three hours long, which felt like an unfair amount of time to subject wild animals to me, so I instead just took a stroll through the animal orphanage, where young animals who aren't able to survive on their own in the wild are taken care of by the park. There, I met Jared, a park employee kind of enough to show me around and even let me pet a lioness in heat, which sounds like a metaphor for something but actually involved me petting a horny female lion through a chainlink fence.

"She won't bite you," Jared assured me.

I hoped he was right. And if he wasn't, I figured, just think of the story!

Jared also showed me a lion named Dave, something I took as a good omen until he also mentioned that Dave had been neutered, at which point I felt Jared might somehow be openly mocking me for my less-than-stellar roller hockey performance with the Ice Lions.

"How could he possibly know?" I wondered before quickly dismissing the whole thing as cruel coincidence.

On my way out of the orphanage, I was thrilled to see a few of the Maasai warriors hanging out by the gift shop. As soon as we made eye contact, one of them waved me over.

"Give me your phone," one of the warriors said as a couple of the others put a Maasai robe on me and a walking stick in my hand as soon as I approached.

Next thing I knew, the Maasai warriors were all jumping impossibly high into the air and making high-pitched noises while the guy with my phone captured the whole thing. I did my best to imitate them, but I mostly just thought about what kind of crazy stuff can happen after you go innocently looking for cool hockey jerseys late at night on the internet.

"Let me give you something," I said once it was all over, fishing my wallet out of my pocket to hand one of the guys the last bit of cash I had on me, the equivalent of about twenty bucks in Kenyan shillings.

"It's normally fifty dollars," the guy still holding my phone said.

"Ohhhh," I replied while slowly backing away after grabbing my phone from him. "Let me see if I can find an ATM nearby and I'll come back."

We both knew I was lying. And since the last thing I needed on my last day in Nairobi was to have a bunch of Maasai warriors on my ass, I quickly disappeared into the café where the comedy show had taken place to drink an espresso while trying to plot my escape.

"You're back," the very same waitress who'd waited on Benja and me on Saturday said as I settled into a table.

"Yeah," I replied. Normally, I'd hope for a compliment at this point, but after my performance at the show on Saturday, I knew it wasn't coming. I downed my espresso, paid my tab and slunk outside into the afternoon sun, where I was delighted to see a group of about fifty schoolchildren who looked to be about six years old, all in matching light blue uniforms seated on a grassy hill in front of the café as what I assume were their teachers set about preparing a picnic for them. It was an adorable sight that at least momentarily made me forget that a handful of Maasai warriors might very well have been looking to exact revenge for my unsatisfactory tip at that very moment. Still, just when I thought my trip to Nairobi couldn't get any more exhilarating, a baboon suddenly appeared and began making his way toward the schoolchildren.

"Oh no!" I thought, assuming I was about to witness something that might very well make the local news.

Then, just as quickly as he'd approached, the baboon snatched a loaf of bread from one of the schoolteachers and quickly made his retreat as all the little schoolchildren and one grown man visiting from New York City began squealing with delight. When I was their age, the most exciting thing that ever happened in school was that they added tater tots to the lunch menu. I'd be lying if I said I wasn't a bit jealous.

I returned to the city a short while later, after a quick detour to go feed some giraffes at the aptly named Giraffe Center. My flight back to New York was leaving later that night, so with the little time I had left in Nairobi, I decided to walk over to where all the matatus waited to take commuters back home after work near my hotel. Part of the fun, aside from admiring all the cool paint jobs on the buses and vans, was having all the matatu conductors try to talk me into climbing aboard if I so much as looked in their direction, as if part of their job was to talk people who weren't planning on going for a ride into hopping aboard anyway.

"And that's how I ended up living in the suburbs of Nairobi," I imagined saying one day had any of them succeeded. And hopefully, there would be a Kenya Ice Lions–themed matatu by then, too.

After the matatu ogling, I met up with Ali and Trevor from

the Ice Lions for a quick dinner at a place called Manhattan Chicken, which felt appropriate, as that's exactly where I'd be by the same time tomorrow.

"Thanks again for letting me play with the team on Sunday," I told them over plates of fried chicken and french fries. "It's too bad we couldn't play ice hockey, though, since I'm not nearly as good at roller hockey."

"Yeah, you kind of sucked, Dave," Ali smiled.

"Yeah, you sucked, Dave," Trevor agreed with a laugh.

Maybe they were joking. Or maybe they weren't. But either way, as I boarded the plane for New York a few hours later, I made a promise to myself that I would definitely return to Nairobi to play ice hockey with the Kenya Ice Lions one day very soon.

And when that day comes, I will absolutely destroy them!

6

To the Beast Cave

I'd never been to Finland before. But when I knew I was going to write this book, one of the first orders of business was to plan a trip to this dark and mysterious Northern European land as soon as possible. After all, not only is Finland the second-biggest hockey country in the world behind Canada, but it was also recently rated the happiest country in the world, no doubt at least partially owing to that thing I just told you about hockey. And when I consider that Finland is also home to more heavy metal bands per capita than anywhere, is one of the world's leading countries in terms of design*

---

* I am not ashamed to say that, as of this writing, I probably have more

and is also where my favorite film director, Aki Kaurismäki,* is from,** it's a wonder I didn't just up and move there years ago to start a new Finnish life for myself.

I should also admit that an additional motivation for wanting to go to Finland was that, given my obsession with hockey jerseys that borders on a disorder according to those closest to me, Finland is also home to the Tampere Ilves (Tampere Lynx in English) of the Liiga, Finland's equivalent to the NHL. I am ashamed to say I was unaware of the Tampere Ilves team and, perhaps more importantly, its amazing jersey when I wrote the earlier, arguably polarizing chapter in this book about hockey jerseys, but I can now say with confidence that it may very well be the greatest sports jersey of all time, featuring what appears to be an equal parts delighted and enraged lynx that looks like it was drawn by a child in the Middle Ages, something I mean in the absolute best possible way. I knew I had to have one for my collection. And while, sure, I could have just ordered one online, I learned that the shipping cost from Finland to New York City was around seventy dollars, almost as much as the

---

Marimekko throw pillows in my home than any other man currently walking the earth.

* If you haven't already, I implore you to go watch as many Aki Kaurismäki films as possible. If you are anything like me, they will ruin you for most other movies.

** I read that Aki Kaurismäki now spends most of his time in Portugal, something I will never understand in a million years, as there is reportedly only one hockey rink in the entire country.

jersey itself, so the very notion of not going to Finland in order to save on postage seemed insane.

Keeping all this in mind, I booked a direct flight from New York to Finland in early October, just a few weeks into the 2022–23 regular season of the Liiga. I wanted to give the teams at least a few games to get their shit together before I showed up on the scene.

I had some time to kill before my flight, so I had a couple beers at a place called the New York Sports Bar just down from my gate. I figured it would be the absolute best spot in the airport to engage people in spirited conversations about Finnish hockey.

"I really think Turku* has a shot this year," I said to no one in particular.

And when that didn't work, I just decided to just take the safe route by repeatedly insulting the city of Boston and its people for no good reason until it was time to board my flight.

The flight from New York to Helsinki leaves in early evening, which would put me in Helsinki proper by midmorning, so I could really hit the ground running. I intentionally flew on Finnair in hopes of experiencing the magic of Finland as soon as possible. I was flattered when the flight attendants all addressed me in Finnish, as I figured this meant I would really blend in over there. And I was impressed when they kept on talking to me

---

* Turku is a city on the southwest coast of Finland, and the former capital. I am told it is also home to Michael Monroe, lead singer for legendary Finnish rock band Hanoi Rocks. But more importantly for the purposes of this book, it is home to Liiga's TPS Turku, the second most successful team in the history of the league, even though their jerseys aren't that cool.

in Finnish, anyway, even after I responded in English, something I took to mean that they both refused to pander and simply couldn't believe I was not one of their own.

On a disappointing note, as best I could tell, Finnair didn't have a single Finnish film in its in-flight entertainment system, so my hopes of binge-watching the work of Aki Kaurismäki, who, together with his older brother, fellow screenwriter and director Mika, is responsible for an impressive twenty percent of Finnish films since the early eighties, were dashed. Instead, I just annoyed the person in front of me by playing Tetris on the back of their headrest before eventually drifting off to the kind of awkward sleep only a middle seat in coach can provide.

•••

I landed at Helsinki airport a character-building eight hours later, ready for what I was sure to be one of the most hockey-riffic weeks of my life, as I'd scored tickets to three separate Liiga games over the course of my visit.

"What brings you to Finland?" the Finnish customs agent asked me.

"I'm going to see some hockey games," I mumbled groggily.

"And what teams will you see?" he replied, perhaps hoping to catch me in a lie and send me straight back to JFK with my tail between my legs.

"I've got home game tickets for HIFK, Tappara and Ilves," I said while staring a hole straight through him and averting an international incident in the process.

"Welcome to Finland," he replied while sliding my passport back to me.

I could tell he was disappointed, yet super impressed.

•••

I had heard Finland is delightful in summer and idyllic in winter. But in October it is mostly overcast and rainy, not unlike my native Cleveland. So, between that and the fact that the announcer sounded exactly like a character from an Aki Kaurismäki film as he emotionlessly grunted out station names, things couldn't possibly have been going better for me as I rode the train into town from the airport.

I arrived in downtown Helsinki about thirty minutes later and began trudging in the direction of the Airbnb I had rented in the Punavuori section of town with my suitcase and a guitar, which I'd brought with me for a couple gigs I wound up booking in Helsinki and Tampere. I figured as long as I was going to be in the neighborhood, I might as well entertain and/or alienate the people of Finland with my trademark not-for-everybody comedy and music while I was at it. It was the least I could do in return for them welcoming me to their country, or at least not stopping me from entering it, to watch hockey games.

My friend Dan decided to join me for the trip and wouldn't be getting in from Los Angeles until that afternoon, so I dropped off my bags and went off to explore a bit. Helsinki is not unlike a lot of other major European cities I've visited, especially in neighboring Scandinavia.* The buildings are older and the streets more winding than in most American cities. The men are taller than most American men, seemingly averaging at least six foot four. I'm six feet tall if I really believe in myself, but I felt like an invisible troll of a man as I shuffled among them. And the women, with their platinum hair and soft features, were so stunning I found myself questioning not only whether we were even of the same species but most of my life decisions. But that's okay, since my primary mission was to watch Finnish hockey, which is much easier to do when everyone in Finland is ignoring you.

My friend Caroline, a Helsinki native who was my neighbor back in 2003 when I lived in the Chelsea Hotel in New York City, was picking up her son from school nearby, so I met up with her beforehand to catch up on what she'd been up to the last nineteen years or so.

"I've never been to a hockey game," Caroline admitted to me over coffee.

"But it's the number one sport in your country, and Finland is the second-biggest hockey country in the world behind Canada," I tried to tell her. "It's your obligation as a Finnish person to go to hockey games."

But she just wasn't having it, so I continued with my wandering shortly thereafter, eventually making my way to the southern

---

* A lot of Americans seem to think Finland is part of Scandinavia, but it totally isn't. Just ask anyone from Norway, Denmark or Sweden, who will all trip over themselves to tell you this while also suggesting that their country is the best country in Scandinavia, even though, in my experience, every country in Scandinavia is the best country in Scandinavia.

edge of the city to stare out at the Gulf of Finland. It was mostly joggers and people walking their dogs passing by as I sat atop the large rocks lining the shore, but I did my best to ignore them as I imagined ancient Vikings approaching from the sea aboard creaking wooden ships, in search of commerce and perhaps a bit of plundering as long as they were in town. And when that ran its course, I stepped into the water itself and bent over to dip my hands in celebration of my arrival in this Nordic and, yes, hockey-riffic land.

"Three Liiga games in one week," I muttered to myself in anticipation of the days ahead as I dug my hands into the pebbles beneath the water for emphasis. "Must be some kind of record."

I continued on, slightly damp, back in the direction of town before eventually stopping into a bar called Tommyknockers, where they happened to be watching an NHL preseason game between the Los Angeles Kings and Anaheim Ducks, something I took as a good omen despite not being much of a fan of either of those teams.

"Are you an HIFK fan?" I asked the bartender while sipping my first Finnish beer.

"I like Jokerit," he responded.

Jokerit is Helsinki's other pro hockey team, and until recently, it was part of the Kontinental Hockey League, which is made up mostly of teams based in Russia. Jokerit left the league in February 2022 in response to Putin's bullshit, aka Russia's invasion of Ukraine.

"I think they are coming back to the Liiga next season," the bartender told me.

"That's gonna rule," I replied, partially because I figured that's what he wanted to hear, but also because Jokerit's jerseys are, with all due respect, much cooler than HIFK's, and feature a jester on the chest, something I guess must disarm Jokerit's opponents, thus allowing them to destroy them more easily.

My buddy Dan had gotten into town a short while earlier, so he met me at the bar and we talked about the days ahead.

"Friday, we're seeing HIFK play at home against Oulun Kärpät," I eagerly told him between sips of beer. "And then Saturday, we're seeing two games in Tampere—Tappara versus SaiPa and then Ilves against JYP."

"Great," Dan replied, still exhausted from his ten-and-a-half-hour flight from Los Angeles.

I neglected to ask Dan if he was a hockey fan before inviting him to join me on the trip, but I chose to believe he was just as excited as I was.

A short while later, we headed out into the Helsinki night in search of sustenance, eventually landing at Ravintola Kannas, chosen partially because they specialize in traditional Finnish food, but also because Aki Kaurismäki, the Finnish director I apparently won't stop mentioning in this chapter, shot a scene from his delightfully murderous 1990 film *The Match Factory Girl* here and I wanted to soak up a bit of the tragic magic. There, we dined on fish and stuff that was mushed in with the fish before jet lag mixed with slight drunkenness prevailed and we were forced to call it a night.

I awoke the following morning, a Tuesday, excited to immerse myself in as much Finnish stuff as possible, which I had plenty of time to do, as the first hockey game of the trip wasn't until Friday. I'd read that Finnish people are really into saunas—so much, in fact, that a quick perusal of Finnish pro hockey merchandise reveals that almost all teams offer a sauna bucket with their logo emblazoned on it. So, in hopes of blending in with the locals, I met up with my buddy Dan at his hotel to pretend that I was staying there, too, and take advantage of the sauna in the hotel basement.

"Is it weird that we're here, sweating together, without a single Finnish person in sight?" I asked Dan as I sat there in a swimsuit I'd bought just minutes earlier at a sporting goods store down the street.

"Maybe," he replied before throwing a bucket of water onto the hot coals. "Maybe."

The sauna was invigorating, if slightly awkward, mostly because the only swimsuit I could find on such short notice was size XXL, and as such, it looked like I had stuck my legs through a garbage bag and just gone with it.

Looking to mingle with the Finns, we decided to cut things short and headed toward the city center in search of an authentic Finnish lunch. At first, we could only find chain restaurants or restaurants serving food that didn't seem as Finnish as we'd hoped—burritos, for example. But then I spotted a small sign advertising a place billing itself as a "Viking restaurant" up a flight of stairs and knew we'd hit pay dirt.

"I bet it doesn't get any more authentically Finnish than this," I said to Dan as we ascended the stairs to the restaurant while conveniently ignoring the fact that, at no point in history, was there such a thing as a Finnish Viking, if you really want to get technical about it.

We entered the restaurant to find a young woman in a burlap dress standing among empty tables, upon each of which rested two plastic Viking helmets, exactly the kind you might pull into service if you were looking to lure two wide-eyed Americans with a taste for adventure into your restaurant.

"What did I tell you?" I said to Dan excitedly as we took it all in. "It's the real deal!"

We were kind of in a hurry, as I had a train to catch to Tampere a short while later, and we also felt sorry for the young woman, as there was no one else in the restaurant. So, we grabbed a table and Dan drank a Finnish beer while watching me eat a delicious mushroom soup I'd like to think would have given me the strength for pillaging later that day, had the opportunity presented itself.

I had a show in Tampere that night with the hilarious Finnish comedian Harri Soinila at a place called Secret Sauceity, an impressively named pizza restaurant that also has comedy shows. The show was a lot of fun, with the Finnish people seemingly enjoying most of my material while also being confused by some portion of it, which is to say it went about as well as most of my shows in the United States tend to.

Afterward, I had a chance to try a popular Finnish beverage called a long drink, which combines gin and grapefruit soda for a taste sensation I couldn't wait to put behind me. I also chatted with the locals about my hot plans to return to Tampere that weekend to see two hockey games hosted by the local Liiga teams, Tappara and Ilves.

"Which team is your team?" a thirtysomething Finnish man asked me as I tried to get the taste of the long drink out of my mouth as soon as possible by drinking a popular Finnish beer called Karhu.

"I don't know," I told him. "They both seem pretty cool."

"In Tampere, you have to choose a team," he stressed to me. "You can't like both."

"Then I choose the Ilves," I declared, based solely on their amazing jerseys, as that's all I really had to go on at that point. "Did you know they charge seventy bucks to ship to America? It's nuts."

It was raining when I woke the following morning, so, while I'd initially planned to explore Tampere a bit in hopes of perhaps staking out a pregame location for Dan and me to get into prime hockey-watching condition ahead of Saturday's games, which is to say at least slightly drunk, I instead decided to just catch a train back to Helsinki.

On the walk over to the train station, I was excited to see Ilves stickers on at least half the street signs, lampposts and whatever else would hold still that I passed along the way, as I love a vandalous fan base. It also made me feel even better about declaring my support for the Ilves team the night before, as notably absent from any flat surface were any Tappara stickers.

"Screw Tappara," I muttered to myself under my breath as I trudged through the rain. It was nice to really lean into taking sides like that.

I arrived in an equally damp Helsinki a couple hours later and met up with Dan at Vanha Kauppahalli, aka the Old

Market Hall, an arcade with all sorts of food vendors that's been in business since 1889, where seniors wandered among the stalls, pointing at various cuts of meat. There, I dined on fried sea bass before regretting that and walking outside with Dan, where there were stalls that sold fish in various forms or souvenirs aimed at people visiting Finland, even though Dan and I, being sophisticates and all, are largely immune to such things.

"In just two days, the hockey games begin!" I reminded Dan excitedly as we stopped at a booth specializing in whimsical hats.

"Can't wait," he replied while regarding a hat that, if worn properly, would give the wearer the appearance of being a fish of some sort—and that, I am proud to say, neither of us purchased, but only because they didn't take cards.

I had a show that night with Harri Soinila and a couple other comedians at Wäiski, a small venue aboard a boat docked off the Merihaka neighborhood of Helsinki. It was another fun show, notable mostly for the fact that a fan asked me to autograph a loaf of bread* for him, an admitted first for me. Afterward, my buddy Dan and I headed out into the rainy Helsinki night in the direction of the bar that was playing NHL preseason games on our first night in town in hopes that they were doing the same thing that night. Sadly, however, they weren't.

---

* In the interest of full disclosure, I should explain that I've made a habit of posting photos of whatever toast I happen to be eating on my Instagram account. I was thrilled that this habit resonated with someone all the way in Finland, to the point that he decided to stop off at the grocery store on the way over to see me perform. Show business is difficult and cruel, but it is moments like this that make it all worthwhile.

For his part, Dan rented a scooter and zipped off for a short while as I held things down alone at the bar, only to return a few minutes later with a damp pizza. There's a certain sadness that goes along with eating damp pizza in a bar on a rainy night in Helsinki, but I also felt like a champion because, as I've been repeatedly reminding myself and you, dear reader, in less than forty-eight hours I'd be witnessing professional Finnish hockey games in person, something I'd like to think I'd worked my whole life for, but had admittedly only committed to a few months earlier.

The following morning, in order to distract ourselves from having to wait for the hockey games to begin, Dan and I hopped a ferry to Estonia, the mysterious land just across the Gulf of Finland from Helsinki, to spend a day in Tallinn. I had hoped our visit would coincide with a home game for Tallin's HC Panter team, who play in the Meistriliiga, Estonia's top-tier hockey league, but it wasn't to be, as their season hadn't begun yet—which is bullshit, but whatever.

Tallinn was lovely and I can't recommend it enough, especially Old Town, a well-preserved medieval city in the center of it all. But let's get back to Finland and finally—yes, finally—some hardcore Finnish hockey action.

I woke early the following morning to catch the ferry back to Helsinki for the first game of our visit, featuring the home team, HIFK, squaring off against Oulun Kärpät. Much to my hockey horror, Dan decided to stay behind in Tallinn to do a bit more sightseeing, which would get him back to Helsinki later that night, but too late to see the game with me. So, I crossed the

Gulf of Finland alone, cursing his name for the first half of the voyage until I noticed a TV on board showing Liiga hockey game highlights, something that brightened my mood considerably despite the fact that I couldn't understand a word the announcers were saying. No matter—hockey is a universal language of skates carving the ice, pucks careening off sticks, and bodies slamming into boards, all of which combine for a symphony to my ears every time.

I arrived in Helsinki a short while later and headed for the Old Market Hall once more, hell-bent on gorging myself on Finnish wonders ahead of the hockey game that evening. I downed a bowl of delicious salmon soup I bought from an outdoor vendor who, coincidentally, was wearing the same whimsical fish hat described a few paragraphs earlier. I also drank an entire bottle of something called sea buckthorn berry juice, a bright orange beverage that, I was told by the guy who sold it to me, was wildly popular with the Finnish people despite the fact that, upon first go-round anyway, it looked much better than it tasted. I expected it to be sweet and fruity, but it was tart to the point of tasting downright poisonous, which I naturally took to mean it must be really good for me, despite the fact that my body fought every wretched sip in the interest of survival. Still, I got it down, as I assumed it would only better prepare me for the nonstop Finnish hockey mayhem ahead.

Since Dan had made the mistake of a lifetime by staying behind in Estonia and causing himself to miss the hockey game that night, I called up my friend Caroline to see if she'd like to join me instead.

"Sure," she told me, barely containing her excitement.

It would be nice to witness Caroline watching the greatest game on earth in person for the very first time in her life and hopefully understand exactly why I'd gotten on the plane over here in the first place.

HIFK plays its home games at Helsinki Ice Hall, aka Petoluola, aka the awesomely named "Beast Cave"* in the north of Helsinki. I made plans to meet Caroline at an extremely non-hockey-themed natural wine bar in the Kallio neighborhood of the city. I decided to stop off along the way at Pub Sirdie, a small dive bar featured in—you guessed it—an Aki Kaurismäki movie, specifically *Calamari Union*, in which fifteen men, all named Frank, attempt to escape Kallio. When I got there, there was no one in the place besides the bartender, so I ordered a beer and helped myself to a seat at the same table two characters from the movie—yes, both named Frank—sat at in this excellent movie I can't recommend enough. And between that and the fact that in just a couple hours I'd be witnessing my very first Finnish hockey game, I felt invincible.

From Pub Sirdie, I continued on to meet Caroline for a glass of wine before we jumped in a cab to the Helsinki Ice Hall for tonight's game between HIFK and Oulun Kärpät, Finnish for Oulu Ermines. Oulu is a city in the north of Finland, along the Gulf of Bothnia, and an ermine, as I've just learned, is a large

---

* The name "Beast Cave" was inspired by an ill-fated earlier incarnation of HIFK's jerseys that featured a big red cat on them for reasons no one seems quite sure of.

weasel-like animal art lovers may recall from da Vinci's *Lady with an Ermine* painting. They also eat mice.

As for the Oulun Kärpät team, they've won the Kanada-malja, the Liiga's championship trophy, eight times—seven since 2004, making them the most successful Finnish hockey team of this century. For their part, HIFK have won the Finnish championship seven times, albeit over the last fifty-odd years. On the plus, side, however, in my expert opinion, they have much cooler jerseys than Oulun Kärpät, featuring a blue and white shield with a star and the year of their formation, 1897, in red. And as you've probably figured out by now, if a team has cool jerseys, I'm probably going to root for them.

As soon as we entered the Helsinki Ice Hall, I was filled with the usual feeling I get when visiting a pro hockey arena for the first time—exhilaration bordering on panic. Exhilaration for obvious reasons, and panic because I'm afraid I might miss something, like a dunking machine or perhaps an opportunity to shake hands with or, who knows, maybe even rub up on a team mascot. But mostly I just love seeing the local team's fans kitted out in hats and jerseys and fans of the visiting team brazenly doing the same on enemy territory, even though it could get them killed. I love seeing what foods and beverages I will be gorging on to help give me the energy to scream throughout the game, often at inappropriate times. And, most importantly, I love getting to my seat, ideally wearing some freshly purchased local team gear that will no doubt be covered in whatever foods and beverages I'd gorged on by the end of the night.

There were just a few minutes until the opening face-off, so souvenirs would have to wait. But I did grab a beer for myself and a glass of wine for Caroline before heading in the direction of our seats, only to find that alcohol wasn't allowed inside the arena itself.

"This sort of thing would cause a riot in the United States," I thought as I attempted to suck down my entire beer in one go like a college freshman on spring break so that we could get inside before the game started.

The Helsinki Ice Hall holds just over eight thousand people and, it being a Friday night and all, was packed with hockey fans who were almost as excited as I was. I'd snagged a couple seats a few rows up on the lower level in HIFK's defensive zone, just opposite HIFK's fan club, easily identifiable by the fact that they all wore the team's red home jerseys and were presumably just as upset as I was about the "no alcohol inside the arena" policy. Part of me wished I had gotten tickets in their section, but, as I didn't have an HIFK jersey of my own, I imagine they would have rejected me on principle, something I would have completely respected.

As the action got underway, the difference between North American and European hockey fans was instantly apparent. While the Finnish fans were a slightly more laid-back compared to the Polish hockey fans I'd witnessed previously, who seemed borderline if not explicitly violent, they were still downright aggro compared to most hockey fans I've witnessed in the United States and Canada, who seem utterly sleepy in comparison.

Particularly entertaining about the Finnish fans is that in

tense moments—when their team narrowly misses a goal, for example—the crowd screams, "Oyyyyyy!" in unison, as if they've collectively been kicked in the gut.

"That's like when Americans scream, 'Ohhhhhh!'" Caroline explained, noting my confusion.

It didn't take long for me to join in and start screaming, "Oyyyyyy!" along with them, and then also sometimes just on my own for no reason whatsoever. It felt good. Really good.

Something else that confused me was the fact that one player on each team wore a shiny gold helmet. Naturally, I assumed that each of these players must just be some sort of jerk, but upon further research, I discovered the gold helmets are worn by the top scorer on each team. Finnish hockey legend Teemu Selänne refers to this helmet as a "Hit Me Helmet," which makes sense as even I, normally a man of peace, had a near-Pavlovian urge to take a swing at the guy in the gold helmet the moment I saw him. The wearer of the gold helmet changes from game to game, depending on which player is on top, which of course now has me wondering whether it's the same helmet being passed around the team or they break out a new one each time the helmet changes hands. These are the things that keep me up at night.

About halfway through the first period, I'd decided that HIFK was dominating the proceedings fairly heavily, keeping the puck in their offensive zone more often than not and simply not putting up with any of Oulun Kärpät's bullshit in general. Still, I wondered if I was just imagining this because it was Friday night in the beautiful city of Helsinki and I wanted things to go well for the home team. I decided to ask Caroline what she thought, since it was her first hockey game and she'd hopefully give me an objective opinion.

"Hey, Caroline," I said, "would you say HIFK is dominating tonight, based largely on the fact that they are keeping the puck in their offensive zone more often than not?"

"Yes," Caroline concurred, making me feel even better about my bold insight into tonight's game.

One detail about Finnish hockey that requires far less keen insight is the fact that pretty much every surface, from the ice to the boards to the players themselves—right down to their butt cheeks—is covered in ads, making the players look like NASCAR drivers on skates. In fact, the golden helmet was the brainchild of league sponsor Veikkaus, a gambling company that figured making the top scorer easier to spot would facilitate fans betting on the games. What with me being a purist and all, I almost wanted to shower just thinking about it. But then again, I guess that helmet does look kind of cool when you get right down to it.

At 15:29 of the first period, HIFK center Eetu Koivistoinen got the first goal of the night with a wrist shot from the left side just outside the crease, causing the Finnish fans, with their relentless chants and oversized team flag waving, and one guy from Cleveland in attendance to go absolutely ballistic.

"No one knows I'm not from here," I said to Caroline with pride as I settled back into my seat after applauding Koivistoinen for just slightly too long. It was exhilarating.

As the final minute of the first period approached, it seemed at least half the people in attendance scrambled out of the arena as if someone had yelled, "Fire!" (or, in this case, "*Antaa potkut!*"). I assumed they were just in a rush to hit the restrooms and get a head start on drinking before the start of the next period. Caroline and I weren't far behind, though I was mostly in search of some sweet HIFK swag that might help me better blend in with the hometown fans and perhaps even infiltrate the actual fan club section. Unfortunately, they were all out of HIFK jerseys in my size, so I just grabbed a T-shirt and HIFK patch I planned to sew on a jacket and wear around town once I got home, in hopes of projecting an air of superiority in my neighborhood, at least in terms of Finnish pro hockey game attendance. I also inhaled an order of french fries I'd bought from one of the vendors, as all that cheering had left me lightheaded. What with this being Finland and all, I'd hoped I could perhaps find nachos topped with herring, but it just wasn't to be.

Things evened out between HIFK and Kärpät in the second period, with both teams managing to control the puck about equally. And, this being European hockey, the familiar hockey sounds of bodies slamming into boards and glass were heard far less frequently than, say, in an NHL game. Even so, this doesn't make the Finnish fans any less voracious. At one point, they began chanting what sounded like "*Eee! Effff! Ko!*"

"What does that mean?" I asked Caroline.

"It's how you say IFK in Finnish," she clarified. "That's what locals call HIFK."

You probably saw this coming, but I began screaming, "*Eee! Effff! Ko!*" pretty much nonstop for the remainder of the second period, the majority of second intermission and then straight on into the third period, where, with the score still 1–0 HIFK, the intensity of the game began to ratchet up considerably. And my relentless cheering totally worked, too, because at 18:07 of the third period, HIFK center Roni Hirvonen ground the puck past Kärpät goalie and, yes, Oulu native Leevi Meriläinen, shortly after which Kärpät pulled Meriläinen and forced him to sit on the bench for the remainder of the game in what I choose to believe was great shame.

As the final buzzer sounded, I took to the streets with my fellow HIFK diehards and continued chanting, *"Eee! Effff! Ko!"* in celebration of HIFK's 2–0 shutout win for at least the next several blocks until Caroline and I got separated from the crowd and my out-of-context chanting began sounding a bit deranged, so I had no choice but to stop so that Caroline wouldn't cross to the opposite side of the street from me.

My friend and disgraced would-be hockey fan Dan had returned from Estonia by this point, so Caroline and I hatched a plan to meet him at the Helsinki institution Sea Horse, a traditional Finnish restaurant founded in 1934 and affectionally called *Sikala*, or "the Pigsty," by those I can only assume stick to just drinks when visiting.

"My friend Andy is here pretty much every night," Caroline told me on the way over, referring to Hanoi Rocks guitarist Andy McCoy.

Unfortunately, however, Andy was nowhere to be seen upon our arrival, dashing my hopes for a Finnish celebrity sighting. All was fine, though, as I was still buzzing from both HIFK's victory and all the beer I'd forced down between periods at the game as a matter of principle.

Sea Horse's kitchen was closed, so Caroline, Dan and I had a late dinner at the place across the street that served decidedly non-Finnish food that I reluctantly ate.

"How was the game?" Dan asked innocently.

"Eetu Koivistoinen had a hell of a game," I told him, referring to the scorer of HIFK's first goal of the night—and the game's MVP, according to some voting I imagine takes place somewhere in the rafters.

"Who's that?" Dan replied.

I looked at him as if he was an idiot, even though I myself had just learned of Koivistoinen's very existence a few short hours earlier. It still felt pretty good, though, what with his foolishly skipping the game in favor of staying behind in Estonia and drinking in its rich and complex history.

"He's only one of HIFK's leading scorers and he's twenty-seven years old and originally from Tampere, the very city we're headed to tomorrow to watch hockey," I then huffed impatiently at Dan. "Gah!"

I thought about storming out of the restaurant for emphasis, but we had to pay the check, so I had to wait, which sucked.

Anyway, I woke early the following morning in anticipation of the trip to Tampere that afternoon. My hotel had a sauna in its basement, too, so, what with me still being in Finland and all, I decided to give it a go in the interest of living as authentically Finnish as possible throughout my visit. But if I thought it was weird sitting in a sauna with just my buddy Dan, it was even weirder sitting in a Finnish sauna all alone with nothing but my thoughts and a possibly unreasonable concern I might keel over from heatstroke at any moment. So, in the interest of avoiding existential crisis, and perhaps even a trip to a Finnish emergency room, which—let's be clear—I can only assume is a top-notch medical experience, I decided to head back to my room after about eight minutes to get myself ready to meet Dan at the train station later.

"Meet me in front of Aseman Wursti," I texted to Dan in reference to a sausage stand that had a name I deemed just funny enough to stand there all alone, giggling about, after I had seen it a few days earlier at the station.

Dan met me a short while later, we giggled for an appropriate amount of time about the name Aseman Wursti, and then boarded the train for Tampere, a city that, as long as we're on the topic, is listed at number twenty-six on a list of 446 "hipster cities" around the world, according to something I read on the internet. Then again, I'm guessing you already had your suspicions about this when I told you I'd done a comedy show there a few days earlier at a place called Secret Sauceity, after which I was later invited to an "after-hours" party by a man who may or may not have been trying to harvest my organs. I guess my point is: do not act surprised when, later in this chapter, I reveal I drank a smoked beer while eating rosemary potato chips at a bar near the arena later that day.

Nearly a week of Finnish/Estonian excitement was catching up with us by this point, so Dan and I rode mostly in silence as we dozed off and stared exhaustedly out the window at the impossibly green, if overcast, Finnish countryside on the ride north to Tampere. But we both perked up considerably as we pulled into town, as the first order of business during our visit was to swing by the Finnish Hockey Hall of Fame.

The Finnish Hockey Hall of Fame in Tampere is housed in a large building that is also home to the Finnish Museum of Games, the Tampere Museum of Natural History and the Postal Museum, where it would have been nice to gain a better understanding of why it costs seventy bucks to ship a hockey jersey to America from here, but whatever. I was excited to see there was also an exhibit called "Monkeys!: A Primate Story" because, duh, monkeys. And I was concerned that there was something going on in the basement called "Tampere in Flames." But since Dan and I had a game to get to, we just headed straight for the hockey museum.

One of the first things you see upon entering the hockey museum is a giant video game of sorts where you stand in a hockey goal situated in front of a large, motion sensor–enhanced video screen so you can try to block shots coming from the 3D players on the screen. I tried to get it to work, but couldn't for the life of me and just assumed the game was broken. But when Dan stood in the exact same spot a moment later and the game worked just fine, I began to question my very existence.

Fortunately for me, however, there were other hockey distractions at the museum, like a room full of Finnish hockey trophies, including the Jari Kurri Trophy, awarded to the best player in the Liiga playoffs. I was especially excited to see this, as Jari was one of my favorite players growing up, owing partially to the fact that I managed to get his autograph out-side the Civic Arena in Pittsburgh when I was a kid, and that sort of thing sticks with you. There was also the *Kultainen kypärä*, or Golden Helmet trophy, which you will be shocked to hear comes in the form of a golden helmet mounted on a stand. Not to be confused with the actual golden helmet the top scorer on each Liiga team wears, this trophy is given to the best player in the league as voted by the players at the end of each season. As I ogled it, I couldn't help but think of Teemu Selänne's remark and how the Hit Me Trophy would be a much cooler name for this one.

Given my jersey obsession, the highlight of the museum for me was all the killer jerseys they had in glass displays, the best of which, of course, was a late-sixties Tampere Ilves jersey, featur-ing the team's awesome lynx logo on yellow fabric that was soiled, torn and frayed after what looked like years of on-ice battle combined with its owner maybe even sleeping in it. Part of me wanted to just smash the glass, steal the jersey and head back to Helsinki immediately, but I resisted the temptation out of respect for Dan, who had a family back home and didn't need the hassles associated with a life on the run.

I slowly and reluctantly backed away from the vintage Ilves jersey to find Dan waiting to play the goalie game again.

"These kids are bogarting the machine," he said as we both stared at four small children all playing the goalie game at once.

"Let's get out of here," I told him as my eyes narrowed in disdain at those damn kids, who, for the record, totally sucked at that game.

Both the Tappara and Ilves teams play at the Tampere Deck Arena in town. The first game of the day was between Tappara and Saimaan Pallo—or SaiPa, as they are known to guys who get it, like me. The SaiPa team hasn't won any championships in its fifty-four years of existence, but has sent seven players to the NHL, which is not too shabby. Still, the Tappara team has won eighteen championships since 1959, so I was pretty much expecting SaiPa to get their asses handed to them today.

We got to the game pretty early, giving us the chance to watch the pregame warm-up, which was more extensive than at NHL games, with teams running countless passing and shooting drills before the game. Our seats were a few rows up at center ice, giving us a good view of any and all action. Speaking of which, there was also plenty of Jumbotron action, as the giant screen featured couples or parents with their children throughout the warm-up. Dan and I were especially entertained by the fact that the Finnish men, without exception, refused to show any emotion whatsoever for the camera, no matter how many times their kids or partners elbowed them.

"You gotta respect it," Dan said as I sat there, desperately wishing the camera would land on us so I could showcase my own lack of emotion, a look I've been perfecting since my early teens at least.

As Tappara and SaiPa headed for center ice for the opening face-off, suddenly the pop music that had been blaring throughout the pregame warm-up switched to the Prodigy's "Smack My Bitch Up," a bold choice considering the many children in attendance, but equally indicative of the open-mindedness of Europeans in general, I figured.

"What's with the guy in the golden helmet?" Dan asked after noticing Tappara's top scorer, Jori Lehterä, shortly after play got underway.

"It's worn by the top scorer on each team," I said to him, as if I'd known this sort of thing for a long time and hadn't found out myself less than twenty-four hours earlier.

"He's a marked man," Dan replied.

Then I told him what Teemu Selänne calls the golden helmet, and we both sat there laughing knowingly for a second. It was fun.

At this game, I also noticed a Tappara player wearing a silver helmet with a giant Red Bull logo, which I soon learned is the U20 helmet, worn by the top scorer on the team under the age of twenty. Suddenly, I felt a bit sad, as the coolest helmet I ever wore at that age held beers. Thankfully, I was distracted moments later as the first goal of the game was scored by Tappara winger Jere Henriksson with a snap shot from the top of the right circle, causing the Tappara fans to go even crazier than they'd already been going since the opening face-off, and causing me to forget the relentless passage of time.

"Tappara! Tappara! Tappara!" they chanted while those seated in the fan club section behind the Tappara goal waved massive Tappara flags. It almost sounded as if they were chanting "Pantera! Pantera! Pantera!"—which was totally cool, as I love that band.

The intensity ratcheted up in the second period, with Henriksson getting his second goal of the night from in front of the net and violence rearing its ugly head in the form of Tappara's Kristian Tanus getting the first penalty of the game, for tripping.

"You get in there and have a good hard think about what you've done!" I yelled as Tanus skated toward the penalty box. But I'm not sure if he heard me.

During the second intermission, Dan and I decided to hit the fancy wine bar they had at the arena, where they actually serve you wine in an actual wineglass. It seemed a little dainty for hockey, but we decided to just roll with it.

"Our seats for the next game are even better than these ones," I told Dan between sips of an organic red.

"Oh yeah?" Dan replied. "When is that?"

"Today," I said. "Right after this one."

"Seriously?" Dan replied, a look of dismay slowly washing across his face.

As it turned out, Dan hadn't been paying attention when I kept mentioning all week that we were going to see two hockey games on Saturday. In the end, he excused himself from the third period to get a bit of a break from all the hockey action, and we agreed to meet up later for the next game, featuring the mighty Tampere Ilves.

I returned to my seat for the third period, determined to scream at least as loud as two men in Dan's absence. And it totally worked, as Tappara forward Veli-Matti Savinainen put the puck behind SaiPa goalie Jere Huhtamaa at 14:59 of the period.

"Jere! Jere!" I chanted. I have no idea if I was pronouncing his name right, but I choose to believe my enthusiasm made up for it.

SaiPa managed to finally get a goal at 10:54 of the third period, thanks to left winger Jesse Koskenkorva, but it wasn't enough as Tappara claimed a 3–1 victory and SaiPa presumably rode the bus back home to Lappeenranta in tears immediately afterward.

As for me, I ran straight for the Ilves team store on the ground floor of the arena immediately after the final buzzer sounded. The game between Ilves and JYP Jyväskylä wasn't starting for a couple hours, but I wanted to get decked out in Ilves gear so I could properly roam the streets and have the smoked beer I told you about earlier in this chapter while blending in with the locals. At the Ilves store, I ended up finally scoring the awesome Ilves jersey I had been salivating over for months, as well as a winter hat, even though it was totally warm outside, both of which I put on immediately.

"Do you have any idea how much I just saved on shipping?" I said with a chuckle to the lady at the cash register as I walked away. I can't help but think she enjoyed the bonus chitchat and probably wished she could clock out of work right then and there so she could come hang out with me. But I guess I'll never really know for sure.

Predictably, the bars, restaurants and streets near the arena were all packed with Ilves fans decked out in Ilves gear, and I was proud to walk among them undetected. I headed back to the arena shortly before game time and made my way to our seats, which were directly behind the Ilves penalty box, almost exactly where my grandfather, my father, my brother Bob and I sat at my very first hockey game, the Cleveland Barons game I told you about. In the inevitable Dave Hill biopic, I imagine it crossfading between these two games. It's going to be amazing.

Whereas Tappara's pregame music was all sugary pop music, the Ilves pregame and between-play music was all hard rock and heavy metal, which added to the excitement. Also, this being a night game, the place was packed. And finally, while the Tappara mascot is just some guy with red hair, the Ilves have the good sense to have someone dressed as a crazed lynx roaming the arena. In short, the Ilves game was better than the Tappara game before it had even started, dammit.

With Dan still nowhere to be found, the puck dropped on the opening face-off, and the first period between the Ilves and JYP Jyväskylä was underway. It was a more physical game than the Tappara game from the onset, perhaps owing in part to the fact that the fans were going absolutely nuts the whole time, chanting, waving flags, the whole deal.

A few minutes later, Dan shuffled down our row to our seats.

"Where'd you end up going?" I asked him.

"I bought a ticket to some Idris Elba movie and took a nap," Dan replied, seemingly refreshed.

It was nice to think that my love of hockey had eventually led to Dan sleeping all alone in a movie theater in Finland, a reminder that anything in life is possible if you just believe.

Back on the ice, the first goal of the game finally came at 1:34 of the first period, courtesy of Ilves center Petri Kontiola, who fired it past JYP goalie Eetu Laurikainen off a rebound on the left side of the crease, causing the Ilves fans, a reenergized Dan and me to cheer in unhinged admiration.

We celebrated further by rushing to the concession area immediately afterward to enjoy another glass of wine, while refusing to be intimidated by all the tall Finnish men also drinking wine in our general vicinity.

"We could totally destroy all of them if we had to," I said to Dan while sipping a crisp white like a man who's not afraid to die.

"Totally," Dan agreed.

The second period held more scoring action, including a breakaway goal from each team, one of which was scored by Ilves U20 Red Bull helmet-wearer Jani Nyman, who got his second goal of the game at 4:16 of the second period. Nyman is just eighteen years old, which naturally gives me an existential crisis mixed with mild joint pain. It's also worth noting that Nyman was picked seventeenth in the second round of the 2022 NHL draft by the Seattle Kraken, so if everything goes according to plan, he will go from wearing the coolest hockey jersey of all time to wearing one of the worst in the very near future. I'm sorry, Jani—you're just gonna have to think big picture here.

During the break before the third period, I began to get a bit sad because I knew I had just one more period of scorching-hot Finnish hockey action before it was time to head back to the United States, where—let me be clear—the fans are pretty much asleep throughout the game compared to the hockey fans I'd experienced so far in Europe. And while the Finnish fans didn't quite have that element of danger the hockey fans I'd witnessed in Poland had, it was kind of nice to know the odds of me winding up in a street brawl after the game weren't very good at all. I guess what I'm trying to say is, I should have just moved to Finland for the entire season rather than visiting for a few days like some damn amateur. Still, we at least had one more period to experience, so Dan and I rushed back to our seats for twenty precious minutes of Finnish hockey glory.

Predictably, the third period between Ilves and JYP was extra exciting, both on the ice and in the stands, where both teams' fan clubs upped the ante on cheering, flag waving and just sort of appearing unhinged in general. As I watched them do their thing, it occurred to me that if I could inject just a little bit of their kind of enthusiasm into my everyday life, I'd probably be the happiest guy from Cleveland on earth.

As for the game itself, JYP swapped out goalies at the top of the period, but it was no use because Ilves center Tommi Tikka just went and scored off a rebound at 17:55 anyway, almost as though he was mocking them. Presumably enraged by this, JYP defenseman Teemu Suhonen scored a few minutes later with a wrist shot from the top of the circle. Then, not to be outdone, JYP's eighteen-year-old winger Joakim Kemell, another one of those U20-helmet-wearing bastards, narrowed Ilves's lead to 4–3 with a slap shot from the left circle.

At this point in the game, the crowd was whipped into a frenzy not seen since, well, the third period of the Tappara–SaiPa game earlier that day. And for a moment, it seemed as if maybe, just maybe, JYP might ride this wave of hockey-based enthusiasm to tie things up. But then, with 1:57 left in the game, they pulled their goalie, enabling Ilves defenseman Leo Lööf, arguably the coolest-named player I witnessed during my entire time in Finland, to score an easy open-net goal from all the way in Ilves's defensive zone as if he were playing for one of those tots teams they let play in between periods sometimes to the delight and/or annoyance of all in attendance.

As I reflect on the last couple paragraphs, it's a wonder I'm not currently employed as a Finnish pro hockey commentator. But perhaps more importantly, I had watched Ilves win, 5–3, on their home ice, which felt positively electric.

I'd naturally hoped to wander the Tampere streets, getting up to all sorts of trouble with fellow Ilves fans, but Dan and I had a train to catch back to Helsinki, so we instead sprinted in the direction of the train station immediately after the final buzzer. We arrived in Helsinki a couple hours later and headed for the city center, where drunken revelers seemed almost entirely unaware that Dan and I had just attended two hockey games in one day—unless, of course, they were paying attention to the fact that I was still decked out from head to toe in Ilves gear.

"I really like Finland," Dan said, reflecting on things as we drank beer and dined on jalapeño poppers, a Finnish delicacy, later that evening.

"More like *Fun*land," I replied. Then we both just sat there, laughing at what I'd just said.

Afterward, we headed back to our hotel and, a short while later, I drifted off to the kind of magical sleep that only comes after having attended three Finnish pro hockey games in less than thirty-six hours.

I woke early the following morning, still wearing my Ilves jersey and winter hat.

"Seventy bucks, my ass," I muttered to myself before drifting back to sleep. "No one gets one over on Dave Hill."

7

A Meeting of the Minds

As you may have noticed, I've spent a lot of time watching hockey, playing hockey or jumping on planes to watch and/or play hockey with fellow hockey lovers in the name of this gravity-defying hockey book. And while I've been having an absolute blast and would be thrilled if my publisher would just allow me to continue this tireless research right on up until my death, at which point some futuristic technology would be employed to extract whatever I'd learned from my brain and neatly type it up into some ideally backbreaking volume, I thought it might be good to take a moment or two to check in with a panel of hockey experts—a quorum, if you will—to get their insights into the sport and also make sure I haven't gone completely insane anywhere along the way in my quest to become one with the greatest game of all time.

With this in my mind, I reached out to a diverse group of hockey enthusiasts, starting with Stephen Brunt, the legendary Canadian sports journalist, radio host and author of the best-selling hockey biography *Searching for Bobby Orr*, among other excellent titles. Stephen has been writing about hockey for roughly forty years, which is to say about thirty-nine years longer than I have. He was also inducted into the Canadian Football Hall of Fame in 2007, something I initially found disturbing for my singular purposes, but which I chose to chalk up to the fact that his hockey knowledge simply could not be contained and, as such, eventually bled over into expertise in another, albeit lesser, sport.

I also spoke with Venla Hovi, who's at least a triple threat in terms of hockey, as far as I'm concerned. Not only is Venla both a former Olympic hockey player and a former professional hockey player, but she currently puts her hockey expertise to use as the head coach of the Metropolitan Riveters, the East Rutherford, New Jersey–based women's professional hockey team that plays in the Premier Hockey Federation. And as if all that weren't enough, she is also from the hockey mecca of Finland, specifically Tampere, where she played for the Tampereen Ilves Naiset of the Naisten Liiga, the premier women's ice hockey league in Finland, which of course means that she got to don that incredible Ilves jersey every single game, about which I am super jealous. And yes, she is also a fan of Finnish director Aki Kaurismäki, so there's that, too.

Finally, I cornered my old pal Dave Schneider, who, it could be argued, is even more obsessed with hockey than I am, as evidenced by the fact that he is the lead singer and diabolical mastermind behind the Zambonis, the Connecticut-based rock band that has been singing about hockey—and only hockey—for nearly thirty years now, including the hockey-based hits "Johnny Got Suspended," "The Goalie Is Drunk" and "Bob Marley and the Hartford Whalers," which is a ska song and not a reggae song, just to keep us all on our toes. Dave even has a Hartford Whalers–themed guitar, certainly grounds for some kind of award—or, depending on whom you ask, perhaps an intervention.

"I was a Hartford Whalers fan, and once this band started, I became more of a fan," Dave told me, as though there's nothing to be concerned about.

The first thing I wanted to ask all three of these hockey experts was what drew them to the game in the first place—an important question, as it would determine whether they "get" the game even half as much as I do.

"I love the sounds of a live game—the skates on the ice and all that," Stephen Brunt told me. "And just to see it up close is amazing—the players today are bigger and faster than ever."

Stephen was speaking my language, as the sounds of the game alone are enough to put me into a trance. I recently bought one of those sleep machines that plays the sounds of a rainstorm, ocean waves, a forest and a handful of other sounds designed to make you feel like you've been dumped off in the middle of nowhere at night, perhaps after a long ride in a windowless van, and none of these come close to setting me at ease the way the sound of, for example, a player being slammed into the glass behind the goal line by an opponent does.

"I love the speed, the physicality and the challenge," Venla Hovi said of her love for the game. "It's really complicated because hockey is not natural for human beings. There's a lot of sports where you run, but then with hockey, you put on skates and you can go way faster, and then you need to handle this rubber puck at the same time."

I was delighted to hear her say this, as it supports my long-held belief that hockey is way harder than any other sport, and thus vastly superior, as you can't just rely on walking and running, things most of us have been doing since we were toddlers— you have to learn a whole new way of moving to play the game, like a squirrel on waterskis, but even harder and admittedly not nearly as cool looking. This fact alone is enough to make it nearly impossible for me to bother paying attention to any other sport without dozing off even faster than I do with that sleep machine.

"I love the beauty of a tic-tac-toe goal," Dave Schneider said, referring to a series of three tape-to-tape passes that lead to a puck in the net. "And I know I have a hockey band and all, but I completely feel that being in a band and working together is the same thing that a team does when they score a goal perfectly."

I wasn't expecting Dave to completely blow my mind like that, but as a fellow musician who also happens to have played hockey most of his life, I realized he was totally right. And once he said this, I knew I could never watch a hockey game— or a band—the same way again, especially a really great band, like Nick Cave and the Bad Seeds or the Zambonis, as just two examples.

Of course, the big question I wanted to ask all of them is the one about why hockey isn't more popular in the United States, or at least not as popular as I, a guy who loves hockey while having an active disdain for most other sports, would like.

"In Canada, hockey is part of our national identity, almost oppressively so," Brunt told me. "Growing up, you had to like it or people would think something was wrong with you."

His words made me jealous. And for the record, I do tend to think there is something wrong with people who don't like hockey, and the people of Canada are not to be faulted for thinking the same.

"There is a financial barrier to playing hockey—more and more, it has become a rich person's sport," Stephen continued. "And you can't just run outside and play like you can with soccer and football, where you just need a ball. So, that's part of the problem."

As he spoke, I couldn't help but think back to when my dad took me to the local sporting goods store to buy equipment ahead of my first season playing organized hockey. I was, fortunately, able to use a pair of my brother's old skates, but I remember looking at the cash register after the guy in the coach's shorts had rung us up and seeing that everything else I would need to play cost my dad $161 and change. It was a paltry sum compared to what it costs to outfit a kid with hockey equipment today, but at the time it might as well have read "a gazillion dollars" on that cash register, as far as I was concerned.

"I better not suck," I remember thinking as my dad pulled out his credit card.

Today, I think about how oppressive the cost of equipment alone must be for so many families hoping to get their kids involved with the sport.

"If you're a parent and you're thinking about what sport are you going to put your kids into, and you see how much hockey cost, it already rules out a lot of families," Hovi agreed. "There's actually a really cool company out of Tampere that started driving around in a hockey bus, selling used equipment for really, really cheap—it's so much more affordable."

Listening to Stephen and Venla, I realized I had been largely in denial of the Occam's razor of it all—the fact that hockey is simply a cost-prohibitive sport, which is likely the primary reason it's not more popular in the United States, rather than some other, less obvious reason I might possibly address by slapping up a few stickers around town to get the word out or something.

"Not as many people in America have actually experienced playing the game, so there's less interest," Stephen added. "They don't have frozen ponds and rinks everywhere like we do here in Canada."

But as much sense as all that makes, Dave Schneider gave an additional perspective on things.

"In America, we say about hockey that you 'just have to see it live' or 'on TV, it doesn't work,'" Dave said. "That's probably not said in Canada or anywhere else."

"Exactly!" I told him. "We use it as an excuse in America. But I don't understand it—I've never had trouble understanding the game on television, even as a kid."

"So, you were not a fan of the glowing puck?" Dave asked, referring to Fox Sports' attempt at getting Americans to understand hockey by making the puck look like a beach ball on TV back in the nineties.

The very thought of it nearly sent me into a blind rage. But it also had me wondering what else my experts think could be done to make hockey more popular in the United States, beyond the obvious solution of making it more affordable.

"I don't want to be anti-American," Dave Schneider began, "but I think Americans would like hockey more if there was more fighting."

The suggestion that hockey, which on the surface, at least, is plenty violent, is still somehow not violent enough for America gave me chills, as I suddenly had visions of some futuristic hellscape where my beloved sport would be combined with mixed martial arts—Conor McGregor on Bauers and all.

"To me, hockey is this ballet on razor blades," Dave continued. "There's a certain amount of patience that one needs to enjoy the game of hockey. And I think sometimes, sadly, that is not the vibe of America."

I agree with the "ballet on razor blades" thing, but I hope Dave is wrong about Americans not having the patience for hockey. I mean, they do watch golf, a surefire nap inducer if there ever was one, so surely there is hope.

"I think growing hockey in areas where it's not popular is really important," Venla Hovi said in support of my quest to make hockey absolutely massive in the United States. "Like, you go to the southern states, some of them have no idea what hockey is."

"I don't know how many people in Alabama get to see a game up close," Stephen Brunt concurred. "I think for Americans to be in a place where hockey really matters makes it easier to become a fan."

With this, I made a mental note to buy a hockey team, move it to Birmingham, Huntsville or Montgomery, and hire Venla Hovi to be the head coach. I am, if nothing else, an ideas man first and foremost. And if I understand Stephen Brunt correctly, it's a solid plan. I can't wait to tell Venla.

"I think eventually hockey will be dominated by Americans—it's headed that way now," Stephen summed up with those words I'd been longing to hear. "It will just take time."

I probably should have stopped consulting my experts right there and ended on a high note. But Dave Schneider wasn't finished.

"They should also make the goals bigger and shrink the goalie's pads down," he added. "That might make hockey a little more interesting, if there's more goals."

Somewhere, Jacques Plante was rolling over—while undoubtedly also making kick saves—in his grave. And it was at this point that I considered hanging up on Dave, but since we both play for Team Hockey Is the Best, I resisted the urge. Also, he said I could maybe borrow that Whalers guitar sometime, and I sure as hell didn't want to mess that one up.

8

The Team Down the Street

I was reading an article the other day about some people in India who got arrested for cheering for Pakistan in a cricket match between the two countries. It was entertaining news, as I love it when people get really upset about stupid things, but also disturbing, as it was emblematic of a problem that goes far beyond the sport of cricket. But more than either of those things, it got me thinking about Kevin, one of my best friends from childhood.

Kevin and I were classmates at Gesu, the Catholic elementary school up the street from my house. And after he moved to my block the summer before third grade, we wasted no time in getting up to all sorts of trouble throughout the mean streets of

suburban Cleveland. From riding our bikes up to the neighborhood deli to get hopped up on candy bars and Coke to seeing if
it was possible to set Bazooka gum on fire in the local woods,* it
was pretty much good times all the time whenever Kevin and I
were together. Until fall rolled around, that is, and things took a
dark turn as Kevin revealed that his favorite football team was
not our fair city's beloved-if-frequently-horrible Cleveland
Browns, but their archrivals, the usually-much-better-at-football
Pittsburgh Steelers.

"Are you serious?" I asked him after he broke the news.

"Yes," he replied. Then he walked inside his house because
his mom had just made spaghetti.

Anyway, as it turned out, Kevin's dad was from Pittsburgh,
and I guess out of genuine enthusiasm, a desire to keep his
allowance coming or some twisted combination of both, Kevin
decided to join him in rooting for the dreaded Steelers, the most
hated football team in all of Northeast Ohio. He and the rest of
his family even wore Steelers paraphernalia around town as
though it wouldn't get them killed at the grocery store or something. I mean, to be fair, it wouldn't, but I can assure you the
stares they'd encounter would be really unpleasant.

Never mind that I didn't even like football and really only
pretended to care about it so the other kids wouldn't think I was
weird, even though I'd already given them plenty of other

---

* It wasn't. The best we could manage was to singe the edges of the gum a
little bit before the matches went out. I love a good blaze as much as the
next delinquent, but it was more trouble than it was worth.

reasons to come to this conclusion; the idea of supporting anyone other than the local football team was unfathomable to me. It almost seemed that, in openly rooting for the Steelers, Kevin was actively trying to tell me to go fuck myself, language we both would have gotten grounded for, to be fair, but hopefully you see my point.

The reason I bring all of this up, of course, is because, as a guy who is not only a hockey fan but also a guy who likes to work the fact that he is a hockey fan into conversation at even the slightest opportunity, I am frequently asked who my favorite team is.

"You must like the Columbus Blue Jackets," folks will say to me. The reason for this, of course, is that I'm from Cleveland, and since there hasn't been an NHL team in that town since 1978, people assume I must root for the team closest to my hometown.

I don't bother pointing out that Pittsburgh is technically closer to Cleveland than Columbus, at least by a few miles, or that—in my experience, anyway—Ohioans tend to dislike, if not openly hate, every Ohio city other than their own, because the real reason I would never root for the Columbus Blue Jackets is that I live in New York City and, as such, feel both a civic duty and moral obligation to root for the New York Rangers, the team that just so happens to play its home games one convenient subway stop from my apartment. I feel like it makes me more of a true New Yorker and more of an asset to my community, unlike Kevin, who is probably terrorizing his neighbors back in Ohio by cutting his front lawn in a Steelers jersey as I type this.

"But Dave," you say, "the Rangers suck."

And to that, I say, "You keep that up and I'll be madder at you than I was at Kevin when he first told me that thing about liking the Steelers. And besides, you don't see me trash-talking your favorite team—unless, of course, you like the Tampa Bay Lightning!" Also, the Rangers don't suck. What are you even talking about? The stats don't lie!

As it turns out, the Rangers and I have a long history together, even though, to be fair, it could be argued that no one in their organization is even slightly aware of it. For starters, I've always been partial to Original Six teams—they're just cooler, and I've got a picture of Montreal Canadiens legend Rocket Richard sitting in a locker room, swigging champagne straight from the bottle, hanging in my bathroom to prove it. But more importantly, after my dad finally broke down and got cable TV for our family in 1981, I was suddenly able to see the Rangers play on television more than any other NHL team, thanks to the bevy of New York area channels beaming into our home. Before long, I was getting as worked up about, for example, a matchup between the Rangers and their rivals the Philadelphia Flyers as anyone in the five boroughs.

Adding to the craziness is that same year, my dad drove my brother Bob, my friend Kevin whom I apparently won't shut up about, and me to Pittsburgh to see the Penguins play the Edmonton Oilers, and it was on that trip that I managed to corner a young Oiler by the name of Mark Messier outside the players' entrance of the Pittsburgh Civic Arena for an auto-graph. Fast-forward to the mid-nineties, when my first band, Sons of Elvis (A great band name? A terrible band name? You decide!), were attending a party we'd been reluctantly invited to by our record label and in walks—you guessed it—Mark Messier, by now a proud New York Ranger, still riding the high of a 1994 Stanley Cup win over the Vancouver Canucks, the team's first Stanley Cup win in fifty-four long years.

"Hey Mark," I asked him between sips of whatever I could get my hands on, "do you remember, um, when I met you in Pittsburgh when I was a little kid, like, a lot of years ago?"

"No," he said politely while understandably scanning the room for someone, anyone else to talk to as soon as possible. "No, I don't."

And finally, at the risk of making your head explode, a few years ago, I saw former Rangers center and, at the time, Rangers TV analyst Ron Duguay crossing Seventh Avenue against traffic like it was no big deal at all.

This is just my life. Accept it.

The reason I bring all of this up, of course, is because I recently surprised my girlfriend, Kathy, by taking her to see the Rangers play—that's right—the Columbus Blue Jackets at Madison Square Garden. It would be our first in-person hockey game since the pandemic, and I choose to believe we were equally excited about it. And, more importantly for the purposes of this important book, I knew it would give me an opportunity to take a closer look at the greatest sport on earth in my own backyard, and hopefully, in the process, gain some insight into why hockey isn't the most popular sport in America, even though it totally should be. I also had a dog to get home to, so there was that, too.

I normally get to a few Rangers home games each season,

usually as the guest of a friend who has a proper job, working for a company that has the good sense to occasionally give Rangers tickets to its employees so they don't revolt. But this time, being a man of the people and all, and also because I couldn't get anyone to give me free tickets, I decided Kathy and I should just head up to the Garden and I would pay for the tickets myself, just like a totally regular person might. We even took the 3 train one stop to get there so as to get into the spirit of things by riding to the game with all the other crazed Rangers fans.

As best I could tell, there were only two other Rangers fans in the particular car in which we were riding. I managed to pick them out from all the other, non-hockey-related passengers by the fact that they were both wearing Rangers jerseys. There was a young man wearing the jersey of Rangers winger Chris Kreider, and a young woman, presumably his partner, wearing the jersey of Rangers winger Kaapo Kakko, who, as long as I'm on the subject, is from Finland, only twenty-two years old as of this writing, and much better than I am at hockey—and probably other stuff, too, I bet. Anyway, I gave them both a knowing glance that I think they would have appreciated, had they been looking in our direction at the time. And for the record, they did get off at Thirty-fourth Street, the Madison Square Garden stop, so I think you'll understand when I say I was feeling pretty good about my detective skills at this point.

Given that the world's most famous arena sits on top of Penn Station, the busiest train station in the Western Hemisphere,*

---

* It's true—I just looked it up.

there's always a certain intensity that comes with attending an event at the Garden, whether it be a Rangers game, a Billy Joel concert or even just a mass wedding,* as you usually have to maneuver through throngs of commuters racing to catch a train to Patchogue, Peapack or some other majestic port of call just to get inside. Still, after a bit of scrambling, and maybe an elbow or two, Kathy and I managed to make it through the doors well before the opening face-off.

As soon as we got inside, we popped into the Rangers gift shop to eye their wares. There, we saw plenty of other Rangers jerseys with the names of various current players on the backs, and I momentarily felt bad for all of them.

"What if no one bought the jersey with your name on it, and it somehow got back to you, maybe even while you were hanging out with all your other professional hockey player friends?" I asked Kathy. "As if making it to the NHL weren't hard enough—now these guys have jersey sale concerns to keep them up at night!"

"These are grown men," Kathy answered. "I don't think they're too worried about it."

"But I'm a grown man and the very thought of it paralyzes me," I wanted to tell her. But she had already moved on to look at the T-shirts.

––––––––––––––––

* In 1982, Reverend Sun Myung Moon married over two thousand couples at the Garden. Just think of all the potato salad they must have had to make for that day. And while, sure, there have been many mass weddings at the Garden, this one is my favorite.

I caught up with her to find a T-shirt that featured all the different kinds of hockey hair styles on it. There were six of them in total, and it turned out I was sporting at least two of them at the moment, which sounds medically impossible, but you just have to trust me on this. And while, yes, I probably should have bought that shirt, we still had tickets to buy, so I grabbed Kathy by the hand and we headed for the nearest ticket window.

"I'd like two tickets to tonight's Rangers ice hockey game," I told the guy behind the ticket window in an effort to make sure he didn't try to sell us tickets to a Phish concert or something instead—file under: last thing I need.

Since, as I already mentioned, I'm a man of the people and also cheap, I snagged us a couple tickets on the upper level—section 211, row 20, to be exact.

"This way we can really take it all in," I explained to Kathy. "The game, the crowd, the intricate and often-overlooked details of the Madison Square Garden ceiling—which, as it turns out, is the only arena ceiling in the world that is concave instead of convex."*

It also goes without saying that, as a Z-list celebrity who has appeared on basic cable television *many* times, I appreciated not having to worry about appearing on the Jumbotron the way I probably would have if I had sprung for tickets on the lower level—and also was a lot more famous. In fact, you can imagine

---

* To be fair, in the interest of wasting time earlier that day, I found myself reading up on Madison Square Garden and was confronted with this startling ceiling-based information.

my relief when the rapper and actor 50 Cent suddenly appeared on screen instead of me during a break in the second period.

"See?" I said to Kathy. "If we had better seats, and also I had any skill whatsoever as a rapper, that might have been us having our privacy absolutely ruined right now."

"Uh-huh," she replied with what I'm pretty sure was a sigh of relief as I took a moment to consider the fact that enjoying the sport of hockey is just one more thing 50 Cent and I have in common.

Backing things up a bit, since we had a bit of time to kill before the opening face-off, Kathy and I ducked into the concession area on the lower level for some snacks, as I had figured this was probably where they sold all the fancy stuff. And my suspicions were correct, as it was there that we dined on mozzarella sticks, french fries and chicken tenders that had been placed under heat lamps mere moments before we snatched them up.

"Tonight we eat like kings," I said to Kathy as I placed our selections under a scanner that somehow recognizes the food items purchased regardless of any extraneous breading, and then the kid in the uniform standing next to the scanner asks you for your credit card. It was like something straight out of *Blade Runner*.

Since it was Friday night and all, I also grabbed a twenty-five-ounce can of Stella Artois, the exact amount needed to get through the first period without having to leave one's seat—unless you are at the game with your girlfriend, in which case you should probably make that can last the whole game so it doesn't seem like you have a drinking problem as much. It's also worth noting that they let you drink it straight from the can instead of pouring it into some lame plastic cup, which made me feel not only seen but also trusted as a grown man who can handle drinking from a can without incident, even after what happened last time.

As Kathy and I made our way to our seats, an odd thing I noticed is how almost none of the people in our section looked like New Yorkers—at least not the ones I'm used to seeing around town and on the subway.

"Where do you think all these people are from?" I asked Kathy.

"Why don't you ask them?" she asked in reply.

And while it would have been a good opportunity to really put my journalistic skills to the test and start asking those in attendance where they were from, I figured having a guy with a giant beer in one hand and a half-eaten mozzarella stick in the other might seem threatening—like a challenge, even—and decided to simply speculate on things instead.

"Eh, probably Westchester," I muttered as we settled into our seats.

Looking back on it, probably the real reason the people at the game didn't look like New Yorkers to me is that so many of them were wearing Rangers jerseys. I realize that might seem counterintuitive; you would think—in a perfect world, at least—that nothing would make someone look like a New Yorker more than walking around in a Rangers jersey. But the reality is, as much as I would be thrilled if the majority of New Yorkers wore Rangers jerseys on a typical day, the only time you ever really see it is on the subway headed for Madison Square Garden on a game day. And even then, it's only a handful.

And while we were initially pretty much the only people in our section not decked out in Rangers attire—unless you count the Rangers T-shirt my girlfriend wore under her jacket, in which case, I guess *I* was the only person not wearing Rangers attire, and therefore part of the problem if anything I just said in the previous paragraph is to be believed—that changed quickly as, moments later, a young man and woman wearing Blue Jackets jerseys sat down next to us.

"Are you two from Columbus?" Kathy wasted no time in asking them.

"Yup," the man replied. "We came up just for the night."

"We're originally from Cleveland," Kathy proudly told him. "I love the Blue Jackets."

"Don't say that!" I said to her under my breath.

"Why?" she whispered back.

"Because we're rooting for the Rangers," I told her.

"I know," she replied, "but I just mean I love the fact that the Blue Jackets are from Ohio."

I wanted to remind Kathy of that thing I was saying earlier, and still completely stand by, about how people from Ohio hate every city in Ohio other than the one they're from, but she had already gone back to making small talk with the Blue Jackets fans next to her, a dangerous game any way you slice it.

Since it was "Essential Workers Night" at the Garden that night, a choir of nurses sang the national anthem before the game, injecting the song with so many lush and soulful harmonies that its melody was rendered almost entirely unrecognizable. But that didn't matter, really, because I could barely hear

it over the presumably drunk guy a few rows behind us, screaming, "Let's go, fockin' Rangers!" repeatedly from the "dawn's
early light" part of the song straight up until the ending.

"That was nice," Kathy said at the song's conclusion, though
I wasn't entirely sure whether she was referring to the choir or
the drunk guy, both of whom were thoroughly entertaining.

The two burly guys in Rangers jerseys behind us weren't
having it, though.

"The way I see it," one of them said in a thick Brooklyn
accent, "it's like 'have some respect for da anthem.'"

"'Zackly," the other guy agreed in an accent that was somehow even more Brooklyn than the first guy's. "It's like, it's great
der showin' support for da Rangers, but wait for da end of da
song ta start yellin', y'know?"

I thought to engage them in a conversation about how there
were arguably too many harmonies in this particular version of
the anthem, but ultimately resisted the urge on the off chance
they might disagree and we'd wind up in a fistfight—a fistfight
over harmonies. What? It could happen.

As the names and faces of the starting lineups for both the
Rangers and Blue Jackets appeared on the Jumbotron above
center ice, I momentarily considered the passage of time and
remembered when all professional hockey players looked like
great big, hairy men to me. Tonight, though, most of the players
looked like children—somehow decades younger than me, even
though it seems like just yesterday that I was practicing my slap
shot out in the driveway in hopes of becoming an NHL great
myself one day.

"Am I dying?" I thought to ask Kathy, but instead took a giant swig of beer in hopes of chasing any and all thoughts of mortality away until at least the second period.

Fortunately, though, the opening puck dropped seconds later and my existential crises were no longer a concern as I was instantly soothed by the familiar sounds of skates carving the ice, bodies crashing into the boards and sticks smacking the puck, ice, other sticks or some heady mix of all three. These are some of my favorite sounds in the world, and I love how you can hear them pretty much anywhere in the arena, even in our humble section 211. Back in elementary school, the sound of a football game on television on Sunday would sadden me because it reminded me I had to go to school the next day (and, as long as I'm on the subject, people would usually yell at me for talking too much during the game, so there's that, too). But the sound of a hockey game has the opposite effect, so much that, even when two teams I'm not particularly interested in are playing, I'll often turn a game on in the background at home as I go about other things, the same way I and all other reasonable people do during *Shark Week*.

"Go, Rangers!" Kathy suddenly screamed as Rangers center Mika Zibanejad, which is to say my favorite Ranger,* headed up the ice with the puck.

I craned my neck slightly to see how the two Blue Jackets fans next to her were reacting to this burst of enthusiasm, but

---

* Not only is Zibanejad a great player, but, like me, he is also a musician, as further indicated by his longer rock hair.

they seemed to ignore it—I'm guessing because they knew what they'd signed up for by coming to the Garden for the game.

"We hate Ohio!" someone suddenly yelled from a few rows behind us.

"Fuck you!" Kathy blurted while still staring out at the ice.

"Who are you talking to?" I asked her.

"The asshole talking about Ohio behind us," she explained.

"But you were just cheering for the Rangers a second ago," I said. "Why do you care if someone talks smack about Ohio?"

"Because we're from Cleveland!" she replied. "This isn't about the game!"

She's a complex woman, and I love her for it. In fact, I was about to consider a subtle shift in my own allegiances, too, but before I could, Rangers center Ryan Strome scored the first goal of the night, and his first of the season, with a glove-side wrist shot fired from between the circles.

"The Mississauga Marauder!" I cheered as a few people in our section turned to look at me.

"Who's that?" Kathy asked.

"Ryan Strome," I told her. "He's from Mississauga, Ontario."

"And they call him the Mississauga Marauder?" she asked.

"Not yet," I told her. "But I'm amazing at coming up with nicknames, and I'm pretty sure it's only a matter of time before this one catches on."

The Mississauga Marauder scored that first goal on Blue Jackets goalie Elvis Merzļikins. The Rangers goalie that night was, of course, Igor Shesterkin, one of the very best currently playing the game. And if there was a hockey game happening anywhere on earth that night where the two starting goalies had cooler names than those two particular guys, I'd sure like to hear about it.

Sometime between the Mississauga Marauder's* excellent first goal and Rangers left wing Alexis Lafrenière's goal three minutes later from the top of the right circle, a guy in a Donald Trump mask sat down in our row, an instant mood spoiler that I ultimately decided to just chalk up to the fact that it was two days before Halloween and, as such, I probably shouldn't get too hung up on such things.

During the break between the first and second periods, the Zamboni came out, carrying some kid as a passenger, which understandably got me a little jealous, as I've been wanting to ride on a Zamboni my entire life, if only for a lap or two. And when they announced the kid's name and even put it up on the Jumbotron, I officially flew into a rage.

"I call bullshit!" I said to Kathy.

"She's twelve, Dave," Kathy replied.

"I don't care—she sucks," I told her while spiraling into a darkness that frightens me as I look back on it now from a healthier place.

Kathy tried to calm me down by suggesting maybe there was a number I could call to arrange a Zamboni ride for myself at the next Rangers home game we attended, but I was too upset to even think about it at this point. Instead, I headed for the concession area to soothe myself by breaking my own rule about

---

* Repetition is key is getting this nickname to catch on.

not getting a second big beer at the game. This time around, I got a twenty-four-ounce can of Dogfish Head Session Sour, as it was the beer that best matched my mood.

On my way back to our seats, I noticed that one nice thing about sitting so high up in the arena is that the ushers don't bother to check your tickets before you head up to your section like they do in the more expensive seats.

"Let's see any of those suckers sitting down in 50 Cent's section try this," I thought as I breezed right past the ushers and climbed the twenty rows up to our seats with almost no noticeable struggle.

The second period wasn't nearly as action-packed as the first, unless you count that it was at this point in the evening that I realized there was a guy in a Joe Biden mask sitting next to the guy in the Trump mask, which only confused me further. Still, I was impressed by their commitment to keeping the masks on, even though it was hard enough to see what was going on out on the ice without masks all the way up in our section. It also occurred to me that maybe they showed up to the game wearing masks like that to try to get on the Jumbotron.

"Who do you think you are, 50 Cent?" I grunted in their direction. But I doubt they could hear me with those masks on.

The break between the second and third periods wasn't as action-packed as the break between the first and second, unless you count the fact that I got to explain to my girlfriend why Rangers fans scream, "Potvin sucks!" every few minutes at random. Okay, fine, I'll tell you, too, in case you don't already know. Here's the short version: In 1979, New York Islanders captain Denis Potvin hit Rangers forward Ulf Nilsson during a game at the Garden, breaking his leg and sidelining him for the rest of the season. Over forty years later, some folks are apparently still pretty worked up about it.

The third period got off to an exciting start as Rangers winger Chris Kreider—yes, the same Chris Kreider whose jersey the guy we saw on the subway on the way to the game was wearing—brought the team's lead to 3–0 by deflecting the puck in front of the net less than a minute into the period, causing the crowd to go nuts in that way a crowd only can after drinking for two periods straight.

Adding insult to Blue Jackets injury, Kreider scored his second goal of the game a short while later, bringing the lead to 4–0, causing me to wonder just how excited the guy in the Kreider jersey we saw on the train must have been at this point and also to feel bad for the couple in the Blue Jackets jerseys quietly sitting next to us.

But my concerns quickly shifted moments later, after someone else in our general vicinity had the temerity to scream, "We hate Ohio!" for what seemed to be the third or fourth time of the evening.

"Say that one more time and I'll kill you and seal your body in the walls of our apartment!" Kathy suddenly screamed.

"That's a bit extreme," I suggested. "And also weirdly detailed, I might add."

"No one talks shit about Ohio and gets away with it," she replied.

As disturbed as I might have been about the whole thing

about murder and stuff, it was nice to look over and see the couple in the matching Blue Jackets jerseys at least take some comfort in Kathy's loyalty to our home state, what with their team being down by four goals and ultimately losing to the Rangers, 4–0.

Shortly after the final buzzer sounded and drunken Rangers fans began slowly making their way to the subway or out onto Seventh and Eighth Avenues to howl in approval of the Rangers' victory, Kathy stood up to shuffle past the visibly upset couple from Columbus in the Blue Jackets jerseys.

"Sorry the Blue Jackets lost," Kathy said sincerely, "but I hope you enjoy the rest of your visit to New York."

"Thanks," they said somberly in unison while staring out at the empty ice like General Robert E. Lee after the Battle of Antietam or something.

As we headed down the stairs, I have to admit I felt a bit sorry for the couple for coming all the way from Ohio to see their team lose like that. And as much as I'm not exactly crazy about the city of Columbus, what with me being from Cleveland and all, and as much as I don't like the Columbus Blue Jackets even a little bit, I still gave the couple in the Blue Jackets jerseys credit for at least rooting for their home team, which is a lot more than I can say for my friend Kevin, a monster any way you slice it. But more than any of that, I guess I mostly wondered how my girlfriend came up with that idea about sealing that Rangers fan's body in the walls of our apartment, even though you know it would mean we'd never get the deposit back. Here's to staying on her good side.

Oh, and as far as gaining any insight into why hockey isn't the most popular sport in America on this particular evening, I've thought long and hard about this, and the only possible answer I can think of in this particular instance comes down to snacks and beverages. At Madison Square Garden, the options for food and drink are practically limitless. Meanwhile, over in Poland, where I witnessed the most enthusiastic fans I've ever seen at any sporting event in my entire life, water, one brand of beer and a lone sheet pizza were as good as it got. Maybe the answer is to keep the fans drunk and starve them to the point of irritability, like lions in ancient Rome, so that they may focus this unhinged energy on the game. I realize this may very well not be the correct answer, but I have decided to call the Rangers' front office about it anyway just in case.

9

The Peterborough Handshake and
Other Canadian Delights

Sometime around my tenth birthday, my dad brought me a copy of the *Hockey News*'s annual yearbook that he'd picked up on the way home from work, and my mind exploded. Not only was the magazine packed with pictures of all my favorite NHL players, but it also featured all the details of their entire careers, like the tiny towns in Canada the majority of them seemed to come from at the time.

"Moose Jaw, Saskatchewan," I thought. "It sounds like paradise."

The magazine also listed all the Canadian junior and minor league teams my favorite players had played for before turning pro. The great Guy Lafleur, for example, was a star forward for the Quebec Major Junior Hockey League's Quebec Remparts before playing for the Montreal Canadiens; Wayne Gretzky played for the Ontario Major Junior Hockey League's Sault Ste. Marie Greyhounds before turning pro as a sixteen-year-old with the World Hockey Association's Indianapolis Racers; and Moose Jaw's own Clark Gillies played for the Western Hockey League's Regina Pats before becoming a New York Islander and winning so many Stanley Cups it was actually kind of weird.

Naturally, it didn't take long for me to start dreaming of one day packing up my skates and heading north to hone my on-ice chops with one of these teams before inevitably turning pro myself. And while none of that ended up even coming close to actually happening, for reasons I'll probably grapple with until my death, I wasn't going to let that stop me from pulling a few bills from the duffle bag of cash my publisher gave me to write this book and using them to buy a plane ticket to Canada to finally catch some of these teams I'd been hearing about my whole life in person. After all, I figured, if I was going to write a hockey-themed book, I certainly had to witness a few games in the actual country where the damn sport was invented, especially games in leagues that are so often the launching pad for future NHL stars. Also, my buddy Nils,* who lives in majestic Kemptville,

---

* In the event that you have already ready my third literary classic, *Parking the Moose: One American's Epic Quest to Uncover His Incredible Canadian Roots* (and if you haven't, shame on you!), you'll no doubt remember Nils from the gripping, and at times even controversial, Merrickville and Montreal chapters.

Ontario, located just a few kilometers south of the mighty Rideau River, told me he'd let me crash in his basement if I ever wanted to come up for a visit, so there was that, too.

Keeping all of this in mind, I had a look at the schedules of the many teams playing within driving distance of Nils' house, put together what I believe to be the ultimate Canadian junior hockey safari, which just so happened to take place during the three days Nils had free to hang out with me, and was on my way.

Given my admiration for the aforementioned Guy Lafleur, poutine and the French-Canadian lifestyle in general, I was determined to start things off with a QMJHL game. And since the Gatineau Olympiques' home ice is within driving distance of Nils' house, I decided to start our adventure there, as the team was playing a home game against the Shawinigan Cataractes the same day I touched down in Ottawa to get this whole thing rolling.

"Gatineau is where everybody used to go to get into trouble," Nils told me shortly after he picked me up from the airport.

"What kind of trouble?" I asked.

"Booze, gambling, you name it," he said. "Their laws are just more lax, their people more . . . free."

I couldn't wait.

As we drove through Ottawa proper, we suddenly found ourselves in front of Canada's Parliament Buildings.

"This is where they had that Freedom Convoy where the guys set up the hot tub outside," Nils told me.

"It's somehow comforting that you guys have morons just like we do in the United States," I replied. "Maybe we're not so different after all."

"Yeah," Nils said while keeping his eyes on the road.

But getting back to the Gatineau Olympiques, prior to the trip, I had done a little research and was excited to learn that the team was owned from 1985 to 1992 by none other than Wayne Gretzky, even though his reps never got back to me about letting me totally hang out with him and get inside his head for the purposes of this book.

"You can not hang out with me and not allow me to get inside your head all you want, 'Great One,'" I thought, "but you can't stop me from paying full price to go watch the team you used to own and now have nothing to do with."

Sometimes you just have to take life's victories where you can find them.

I assumed we'd just drive back to Kemptville after the game that night, but Nils suggested he wanted to drink deep from the chalice of glorious Gatineau, so I booked us a couple rooms at the second-classiest motel in town, which, in keeping with what Nils had told me about the town earlier, was located directly across the street from a gentlemen's club, or "peeler bar," as I am told the people of Canada are wont to call them.

"What'd I tell you about Gatineau?" Nils said with a smile as we entered our adjoining rooms that not only opened up right into the parking lot, but arguably combined to form one big suite if we both kept our doors open and didn't have hang-ups about walking outside to get back and forth throughout our stay.

I suppose I should mention at this point that Nils and I, while both the very definition of gentlemen, had no intention of visiting the gentlemen's club literally no more than a hundred feet from

our motel room doors, even though, according to the joint's website, it was the number one gentlemen's club in the entire Ottawa-
Gatineau area and had no fewer than thirty separate champagne
rooms, which seems like a lot if you consider that men, when
gathered in large numbers, almost never drink much champagne
in my experience, or at least not enough to require an entire room
dedicated to its consumption. I guess my point is that Nils and I
had come to Gatineau to watch hockey, and that's exactly what we
intended to do, no matter how hard the gentlemen's club across
the street from our motel was trying to be the very best at its job.

Since we wouldn't be partaking in any champagne rooms,
however, Nils and I figured we should at least head for the
nearest SAQ, or Société des alcools du Québec, to load up on
drinks to enjoy in and/or directly outside our motel rooms
before the game.

"Who needs a champagne room?" I said, cracking open a
tall boy of beer on the sidewalk in front of Nils' room a short
while later.

"Exactly," he replied before taking a swig of room-temperature vodka straight from the bottle. "We gentlemen are having
way more fun right here. At a motel in Gatineau."

Adequately primed for hockey just a short while later, Nils and
I took a cab over to the Centre Slush Puppie,* the Olympiques'

---

* You may have guessed this already, but this is French for Slush Puppie
Center. And if you're like me and had assumed up until now that the Slush
Puppie people didn't do the kind of business that would allow them to have
an entire hockey arena named after them, the giant dog holding a Slush
Puppie on the side of the building will tell you different.

home arena, where I was delighted to find they were offering Bloody Caesars, the official liquid of Canada, as they are illegal in my native America.*

"You can really taste the clam," I said to Nils as I settled into my seat with a large plastic cup of the delicious, bivalve-based Canadian nectar.

"Yeah," Nils agreed.

Before the game itself got underway, a man in a coat and tie shuffled onto the ice to say a few words in French while the Olympiques' mascot, Hully, a dog of some sort, sat in a folding chair at center ice and pretended to be so bored at the man's words that he was falling asleep, something I and rest of the crowd really seemed to get a kick out of, as you can imagine.

"This is like going to German church," Nils said of the fact that everyone in the place besides us seemed to be speaking French. "I just don't know what's going on."

"We understand hockey," I reminded him. "And that's what matters."

Moments later, the puck was dropped for the opening face-off and Shawinigan began dominating the proceedings with lots of crisp passing and keeping of the puck in their offensive zone. I might add that their jerseys were much cooler than Gatineau's, featuring an irritated-looking Indigenous chief on the chest, even though *cataracte* apparently means "waterfall" in French.

---

* Not really. But Americans tend to have a collective aversion to any beverage using clam in liquid form, so, regrettably, the Bloody Caesar is almost nowhere to be found in my primitive homeland.

Personally, I'd like to see a Shawinigan jersey with an irritated-looking waterfall on the chest, as I respect a design challenge, but, regardless, it can't be denied that the team's bright yellow jerseys are much more fetching than the Olympiques' relatively boring black, silver and white jerseys, which were apparently inspired by the almost-as-bad Los Angeles Kings jerseys from when that Kid Rock fanboy Gretzky owned the team.

However, Shawinigan's vastly superior jerseys weren't enough to give them a clear edge over the Olympiques, as the score remained 0–0 at the end of the first period.

"That's the most intense job in Canada right there," Nils said as the Zamboni rolled onto the ice during the first intermission. "Everyone's counting on you."

"Yup," I agreed. "And you've got to do it while just praying the thing doesn't burst into flames while you're out there."*

"Exactly," Nils replied. "You never know which lap might be your last."

As the second period got underway, it occurred to me how laid-back the fans at this game seemed in comparison to the games I'd attended just a few weeks earlier in Poland, where the fans' enthusiasm bordered on violence at all times, even in between periods while waiting in line for snacks. You'd think Canadian hockey fans would be the most enthusiastic in

---

* In 2020, a Zamboni in the Rochester, New York, area burst into flames while cleaning the ice at Bill Gray's Regional Iceplex. And if you don't think the threat of fire hasn't been in the back of mind of every Zamboni driver out there since, you are completely deluding yourself.

the world, given that the sport was invented in their country, but it just doesn't seem to be the case. In short, get it together, Canada!

Despite their relatively relaxed fans, the Olympiques scored the first goal of the game during a Gatineau power play midway through the second period with a nice snap shot by defenseman Cole Cormier from the top of the left circle.

"That's it, Gatineau—rain hellfire on those damn Cataractes!" I screamed while banging on the empty seat in front of me after the puck went in the net. But no one besides Nils seemed to really notice.

"You okay there, Dave?" Nils asked.

"Yes, I'm fine!" I screamed at him, hoping my enthusiasm might rub off on at least the other people in our section. "Why do you ask?!"

As the clock ran out on the third period, it became apparent—at least to me, anyway—that all my cheering had really paid off, as the Olympiques were up, 2–1, causing the Cataractes to pull their goalie in the final minute or two of play.

"I get so stressed out when teams do that," I said as the Cataractes tried to even the score with six skaters on the ice. "It usually backfires and the other team just gets an empty-net goal!"

"You gotta give 'er!" Nils said, suddenly matching my enthusiasm for the first time in the game.

In the end, though, neither team managed to put the puck in the net again, and the final score remained 2–1. It's at this point that I'd hoped everyone in attendance would run out into the Gatineau night to celebrate wildly and, who knows, maybe even wait until the Shawinigan players were headed for their bus so they could give them the finger, but instead everyone just exited the Centre Slush Puppie so quietly, you'd think they were coming out of a Joann Fabrics or something.

As for Nils and me, we hopped in a cab in search of whatever French-Canadian delights this town might have to offer (you know, aside from the gentlemen's club across the street from our motel, the number one club of its kind in the entire Ottawa-Gatineau area), which, on this particular rainy Quebec night, turned out to be some questionable poutine at some bar located in a strip mall, followed by a brief stop at a bar hosting an extremely drunken open mic night, and ending at yet another bar, where the bartender and a French-Canadian chef named Rafael made solid arguments to us about how the first two places we went after the game "sucked," something that sounded much cooler than normal, thanks to their French-Canadian accents.

Our night concluded back at the motel, as I reveled in having finally got to see a QMJHL game in person and Nils swigged more room-temperature vodka straight from the bottle while smoking a Canadian cigarette in the parking lot in front of our rooms.

"We really did it, Nils," I said as I sat in a chair positioned near the doorway of his room so I could keep an eye on him.

"Yup," Nils agreed. "I feel alive!"

Despite Nils' feelings of vitality, I was concerned that we might have squeezed a little too much fun into one evening and he might not, in fact, survive the night. So, I was thrilled when I woke up to the sound of coughing coming from his room the following morning, especially since I'd already gotten us tickets to two more hockey games in the next forty-eight hours.

After grabbing breakfast at a diner not far from our motel (or the number one gentlemen's club in the entire city of Ottawa-Gatineau area, for that matter), where an elderly French-Canadian man asked in both French and English if I minded if he peed next to me, thus making the proceedings all that much more awkward, Nils and I hit the road for the next stop on our hockey expedition: Peterborough, Ontario. It was there that we'd be catching a late-regular-season home game between the Ontario Hockey League's Peterborough Petes and the Kingston Frontenacs.

"Hey, Dave, aren't the Peterborough Petes the same team Wayne Gretzky played on for a whopping three games during the 1976–77 season before he played for the Sault Ste. Marie Greyhounds?" you ask.

And to that I say yes, they are. And as thrilling as that bit of trivia definitely is, the main reason I was so excited to see the Petes play in person was that I'd be watching the game with former Petes head coach Dick Todd, who is not only the winningest coach in Petes history but also a former assistant coach for the New York Rangers, the team that plays just twenty-odd blocks from my apartment.

Given his impressive hockey résumé, I was admittedly a bit nervous to meet Dick Todd in person, but Nils set me a bit more at ease by distracting me during the three-and-a-half-hour drive to glorious Peterborough.

"Did I ever tell you about Kemptville roulette?" Nils asked me somewhere near Sharbot Lake.

"No," I said. "What's that?"

"Five guys each have a beer," he said. "Four of the beers have a Viagra at the bottom and the other has a roofie in it."

"Then what happens?" I asked.

Nils didn't answer, but the very thought of it had my mind absolutely racing for the next couple hours at least, until Nils, for some reason, made the absurd claim that basketball was invented in Canada* and I had something else to get distressed about.

Shortly after we crossed the Frontenac Axis, Nils and I drove past an axe-throwing establishment, and Nils, an arborist by trade, couldn't help but perk up a bit.

"I don't understand why people pay to do that," Nils mused, "though I guess when you cut down trees for a living, you don't want to take your work home with you."

"Yeah," I agreed. "It would be like Connor McDavid shooting pucks out in the driveway or something."

"Exactly," Nils said. "It would be insane."

"Totally insane," I agreed. "Then again, it probably would help him stay sharp."

"True," Nils replied. "He probably does shoot pucks in the driveway, the more I think about it."

Nils kept driving. And as the dulcet tones of Canada's own Kim Mitchell poured from Nils' car stereo, we finally arrived in

---

* As it turns out, the guy who invented basketball, James Naismith, was born in Almonte, Ontario, thus Nils' confusion. But he waited until he was in Springfield, Massachusetts, some years later to come up with a sport I am not only uninterested in but am so bad at, it's almost impressive.

Peterborough proper, where I had arranged for us to stay at a bed and breakfast located above a plant nursery, something that was every bit as charming as it sounds, assuming you like plants, mulch, gravel and other things commonly associated with the plant nursery lifestyle.

Nils and I were just getting settled when his friend Terry arrived from Toronto to join us for this leg of our Canadian hockey odyssey.

"I placed an ad the other day on a website, asking to watch a couple have sex," Terry volunteered mere minutes after walking through the door.

"Why would you need to see that sort of thing in person?" I asked. "Can't you just watch stuff like that on the internet if you're so inclined?"

"Well, we just drove all the way to Peterborough to watch a hockey game in person when we probably could have just watched it on TV somehow, I bet," Nils countered.

I don't know if this was one of those "teachable moments," or if Terry was just some perverted angel somehow sent to remind us of the importance of our mission of watching Canadian hockey games in person or what, but between that thing about Kemptville roulette, Nils' ridiculous basketball claim and this latest bit of news from Terry—a man I had just met but apparently set at ease almost immediately, based on his comfort level at discussing just about anything, it would seem—I was feeling a bit rattled.

"Guys, I'm watching the game tonight with the winningest coach in Peterborough Petes history," I told them. "I really need to focus and not talk about Terry watching people have sex a second longer."

"What if Dick Todd makes you do some drills while you're hanging out with him?" Nils asked.

"Like what?" I asked.

"Wind sprints, puck control exercises, that sort of thing," Nils replied.

I'd admittedly not thought of that. And now I had one more thing to be rattled about.

As game time approached, Nils, his perverted friend Terry and I took a cab into town, where we stopped off at a hockey-themed bar across the street from the Petes' home ice called the Stick to get pumped for the game along with a bunch of other people who were at least as excited about hockey as we were. It was nice to be hanging out in such a hockeycentric environment, as this sort of situation is harder to come by in the States.

"I'm the only guy in my neighborhood who even wears hockey jerseys," I lamented to Nils and Terry, in hopes of getting a little sympathy as we settled around a table.

"Sounds like a pretty cool neighborhood," Nils replied.

I couldn't tell if he was being sarcastic or not. And I figured I wouldn't bother asking him, since he drove us all this way. But more than either of those things, I was getting nervous about the game, so I decided to leave Nils and Terry to their pregaming and head over to the arena a little early to meet up with Dick Todd.

I entered the arena through a cool side entrance used by press, scouts, people from the Petes organization and, on this particular Thursday, guys from Cleveland. I told the first person I saw I was there to see Dick Todd and was led into a room where Dick and assorted Petes coaching staff were seated around a table, talking about what I can only assume was something related to hockey.

"Hey, I'm Dave," I said with a wave, "the guy writing the hockey book."

I realize this is my own hang-up, but as I stood there and they all turned their heads in my direction, I instantly felt like I was back in high school and a table full of cool kids were sizing me up in the cafeteria. And I was especially questioning whether or not I should have removed the brooch from my jacket before I got there, as I just wanted to seem like a cool guy who was really into hockey on this particular night and not necessarily a guy that somehow manages to be effortlessly fashion-forward at every turn. Fortunately, Dick immediately made me feel at ease as he stood up and said hello.

"Let's head upstairs," he said, leading me to a special area of the arena where NHL scouts and other hockey cognoscenti watch the game.

As we entered the scouts' area, it was clear that Dick is royalty in these parts from the way everyone in the room turned to greet him warmly. I was especially excited to be watching the game from what felt like the inner sanctum, but also nervous as the representatives of the Petes I'd been in contact with told me I shouldn't approach any of the scouts or cheer during the game.

"That's Jeff Beukeboom over there," Dick told me, nodding to the very tall former-Edmonton Oilers and New York Rangers defenseman jotting down notes as we settled into our seats high above the Petes goal.

"M-m-must n-not approach J-jeff B-beukeboom," I thought as I resisted the urge to run over and grab a selfie, or perhaps offer him some leftover trail mix I had in my pocket before the opening face-off.

Dick currently works as a senior advisor for the Peterborough Petes, but started with the team back in 1973 as a trainer before working his way up to head coach in the 1980–81 season and continuing in that position through 1992–93. He returned as head coach for two years in 2004 and remains the winningest coach in Petes history, with three OHL championships under his belt.

As if all of that isn't enough, his time as an assistant coach with the New York Rangers from 1993 to 1998 coincided with the team's first Stanley Cup win in over fifty years in 1994. In short, I really hoped I wouldn't say anything too stupid while watching the Peterborough Petes with him.

"So, you got started in hockey as a goalie?" I asked him in reference to something I'd read on some random hockey website in preparation for our meeting.

"No, I was a baseball player," he told me. "There's some misinformation on the internet—I never played much hockey."

I was already feeling stupid. Dammit.

As the game got underway, Dick started schooling me on the OHL.

"Most of the players are between sixteen and twenty years old," he explained. "Each team only gets to have three players over twenty."

What with me being a few decades past my twentieth birthday already, I could feel my OHL dreams officially slipping away after he told me that last part.

Many of the Petes players, in fact, were still in high school.

"When I was the coach, I would call their school every day to make sure they were in class," he explained. "And if they skipped school, they wouldn't suit up for the next game."

As for the game itself, it was much scrappier than we'd seen the night before in Gatineau. There were a lot more goals, too, with the first period ending with the Petes and Frontenacs tied at 3–3.

"It's harder to coach in the OHL than the NHL because these guys just want to score goals," Dick explained. "But you have to get them to play defense, too, or they won't make it to the NHL."

During the break after the first period, I couldn't resist asking Dick about his time with the Rangers.

"I came up with a drill the Rangers would do called the 'double whammy,'" Dick told me before describing a skating exercise that would kill most people, in which the players would repeatedly skate from the goal to center ice and back, then to the opposite goal line and back as fast as they could. "We were doing the double whammy during the preseason when Messier was captain, and he was beating all the younger players in the drill."

"Awesome," I replied, excited to hear some Mark Messier talk, as he is one of my favorite players ever.

"That's when I knew we were going to have one hell of a year," Dick continued. "Messier is a great leader."

"And what was it like having Gretzky on the team?" I asked.

"He was always the first one at practice every day," Dick recalled. "He'd show up early and watch game tapes in my office."

I decided this would be a perfect time to tell Dick about the time I met Mark Messier and Wayne Gretzky when I was eleven.

"The Oilers were playing the Pittsburgh Penguins, so I waited outside the Civic Arena and got their autographs on a program," I told him. "I still have it somewhere."

To his credit, Dick nodded and smiled politely. But it was in that moment that I realized that a guy who'd coached both of those guys at the highest level of hockey in the entire world might not necessarily have been all that impressed with my story.

As long as we were talking about the Rangers, though, I decided to ask Dick why, as best I could tell, so few Rangers players ever actually live in New York City, thus making it next to impossible for me to stalk them at the grocery store, neighborhood restaurants or any of the other places I usually like to corner strangers.

"The Rangers' practice facility is in Rye, New York, so most of the guys usually live up there," Dick explained. "It's easier to get to practice."

So much for hitting my neighborhood Bed Bath & Beyond with Mika Zibanejad and Chris Kreider, whether they like it or not. Ah, well.

What with Dick being a guy who has coached at the highest levels in both Canada and the United States, I thought maybe he could help me with my eternally nagging question about why hockey isn't more popular in the United States, when—I think we can all agree—it should definitely be the number one sport.

"You have to remember we started off with just six NHL teams, and that wasn't that long ago," Dick told me. "But hockey is growing in the United States every year—it'll get there."

As Dick said these words to me, I kind of felt like we were in an alternate universe, a more hockeycentric version of the old TV series *Kung Fu*, and the master was telling this grasshopper he just needed to be patient. I'm not gonna lie—it felt pretty awesome.

As the second period got underway, Dick brought my attention to the Frontenacs' star center, Shane Wright.

"He's eighteen years old and he's the number one NHL draft pick* in the entire world," Dick explained. "People have been talking about him nonstop since he was twelve years old."

I couldn't help but try to think back to my biggest accomplishment at the age of twelve, and all I could come up with is being able to play the main riff to Deep Purple's "Smoke on the Water" on one string on my dad's old nylon-string guitar—which, the more I thought about it, was cool, but maybe not as cool as being the twelve-year-old hockey phenom that people wouldn't shut up about.

Despite all the hype around Wright, the star out on the ice this particular evening was Petes left wing Joe Carroll, who scored a hat trick to lead the Petes to a 6–4 victory over the Frontenacs.

------

* As it turned out, not long after this particular game, Shane Wright was selected fourth overall in the 2022 NHL draft by the Seattle Kraken. Maybe he can do something about those jerseys.

As we headed out of the scouts' area, Dick paused and pointed toward all the conference and league championship banners hanging behind the team benches.

"See all those?" Dick asked with a smile.

"Yup," I replied, noting the years on each of them. "You were head coach for the majority of those."

Then we walked out of the scouts' area while I continued to resist the urge to pester Jeff Beukeboom.

"I was a baseball player who ended up having a career in hockey instead," Dick said, modestly summing up his amazing coaching career as we headed for the elevator.

After I thanked Dick for letting me join him for the game and we said our goodbyes, I decided to swing by the Petes gift shop for a souvenir, which is where I found a wobbly Nils and Terry already wearing Petes toques with the tags still on them.

"You got to take a whole hockey game off from debauchery," Nils said with a slur as I stared at the two of them in judgment, "but I had to go into the bathroom and do shots of Jameson with Terry all night."

After I took a moment to feel grateful about not asking the Petes organization if Nils and Terry could join me in watching the game with Dick Todd that night, we headed back over to the Stick for what I assumed would be a raging postgame victory celebration with all the jersey-clad Petes fans who'd been hanging out at the bar before the game. Instead, however, we found the place mostly empty, except for the bartender and a couple guys who looked like they could be extras from *Duck Dynasty* sitting at the bar.

"Did you hear about the 'Peterborough handshake' yet?" Paxton, the bearded and tattooed bartender, asked me after I'd told him it was my first time in this beautiful area.

"What's that?" I asked.

"It's a sucker punch," he replied.

Between Kemptville roulette and the Peterborough handshake, I was starting to think Ontario was a lot more nuts than I had ever imagined. And as we left the Stick a few sips later, I made a mental note to watch my back, while also considering taking a swing at Nils or Terry when they weren't looking at some point before we split town, just in the interest of fitting in.

We awoke the following morning, said our goodbyes to Terry while wishing him the best in achieving his internet classified goals, and pointed the car in the direction of Kemptville, where that night there was a Central Canada Hockey League Junior A game between the Kemptville 73's and the Renfrew Wolves. The original plan was for Terry to join us after stopping back home, but later that day, he texted Nils to say he had "puked up a crayon" and wouldn't be attending. I decided it was best not to question whether the thing about the crayon was true, or perhaps just a euphemism for something much worse, and instead did my best to focus on the evening ahead.

After a power nap in Nils' basement, he and I headed to a diner in town for our pregame meal, where we were seated by a waitress named Laurie.

"Her husband used to live with Tie Domi," Nils told me after Laurie showed us to a booth.

"You mean Tie Domi the former Maple Leafs enforcer?" I asked.

"Yes, Tie Domi the former Maple Leafs enforcer," Nils said, opening a menu.

"Does she ever talk about what Tie was like as a roommate?" I asked. "You know, whether or not he was messy, or what kind of snacks he liked when he wasn't enforcing, and that sort of thing?"

"No," Nils replied.

It was exactly this sort of juicy hockey-related conversation that made me want to visit Canada for the purposes of this book in the first place.

What with Terry's alleged crayon incident and all, we had an extra ticket for the game that night, so we swung by Nils' friend Brian's house in the woods to see if we could tempt him with a night of red-hot Canadian Junior A hockey action.

"But I'm listening to Chilliwack tonight," Brian said, in reference to the Vancouver-based rock ensemble, after we barged through his front door and made the offer.

"Chilliwack can wait," Nils said as we waited for Brian to put his shoes on.

In Brian's minor defense, I will admit that, up until that point in my life, I had only been familiar with Chilliwack's hit song "My Girl (Gone, Gone, Gone)," arguably the only one of the band's songs to put a significant dent in the psyche of the American people as it reached number 22 on the *Billboard* Hot 100 chart shortly after its release in 1981. But to Brian's—and, by extension, the band's—credit, the sounds of Chilliwack I was exposed to in his house while waiting for him to get ready to come to the game made me realize that the band has a diverse and inspired catalog that goes far beyond that one song that was on the radio back in Cleveland when I was a kid. Even so, we had a hockey game to attend, so as soon as Brian had fully steeled himself for the night ahead, we were out the door.

As for the Kemptville 73's, the team was formed in 1969 and were originally known as the Kemptville Comets until 1973, when they decided to change the name to the 73's for reasons I will never understand, beyond the possibility that maybe they were just really into that particular year. I will, however, allow that their logo, while not nearly as violent-looking as I prefer hockey team logos to be, is still pretty cool.

The Kemptville 73's play their home games at the North Grenville Municipal Centre, which looks just like your average local ice rink, right down to the hockey moms selling tickets and team merchandise behind folding tables at the rink entrance. It was there that I spotted game-used 73's jerseys priced to move at around forty bucks American. And if you think I didn't buy one and put it on immediately so as to appear to be one of the biggest Kemptville 73's diehards in the building, you are out of your mind.

After I scored the jersey, Brian, Nils and I made our way inside and grabbed a seat about five rows up in Kemptville's defensive zone, where the familiar and intoxicating funk of a hockey rink slowly began to fill my nostrils. Also, you could tell a lot of the 73's fans in our section were wondering who the hell Nils and Brian were as soon as we sat down, but, on account of my 73's jersey and all, the hometown fans immediately accepted me as one of their own and it felt amazing.

"Go number 10! Go number 10!" I began screaming. At that point, I had no idea whether whichever Kemptville 73's player wore number 10 was even on the ice, or if anyone on the team was even wearing the number 10 on his jersey that night. But since it was the number on the back of the jersey I'd just paid cold, hard Canadian cash for, I figured I might as well lean into things, and it felt good.

"There's gonna be a scrap tonight," Nils suddenly said.

"You mean because I'm screaming too loud?" I asked.

"No, I mean out on the ice," Nils clarified.

"You can feel it, right?" Brian said, leaning toward the ice as though he really hoped Nils was right about the potential for on-ice violence that evening.

While there wasn't a fight in the first period, it was definitely a more physical game than either of the QMJHL or OHL games we'd seen the previous two nights. Also, for what it's worth, the arena was at least ten degrees colder than the other two Nils and I had just been to, so I was grateful to be wearing an extra layer in the form of the used Kemptville 73's jersey I'd just bought—which, as long as I'm on the topic, didn't smell like it had been washed since the last time it saw on-ice action, either. Not that I was complaining—the nimbus of stale body odor, dried spit and Gatorade emanating from the jersey just proved to me it was the real deal and my money was indeed well spent.

Renfrew's Christopher Hocevar managed to score the first

goal of the night, disappointing the majority of the 236 people in attendance, including Nils, Brian and me—Nils and Brian because they both live in Kemptville, and me because I'd just bought that jersey and felt like I'd already spent too much money to remain neutral on the proceedings. And speaking of the jersey yet again, I was happy to learn later in the first period that number 10 was worn by 73's defenseman Evan Beaudry, who, according to the team's website, is an inch taller than I am and about ten pounds heavier. That said, Evan, if you're reading this, I look absolutely amazing in your jersey, and I don't think anyone seated in our section that night would argue with me about that one bit.

Late in the first period, Canadian national treasure Bryan Adams's "Summer of '69" began blaring from the rink sound system, presumably in the interest of keeping both the players and the fans pumped for the scorching-hot CCHL Junior A hockey action at hand.

"That's a little bit of CanCon for you," Brian said to me.

"What's CanCon?" I asked.

"Canadian content," Nils clarified.

"Yeah, it's the law that a certain percentage of the music played in Canada has to be by Canadian artists," Brian told me.

I'm not necessarily a Bryan Adams fan, and I would have much preferred to hear CanCon-approved Broken Social Scene, Cauldron, Danko Jones, Damhnait Doyle, Fucked Up, David Myles, Brutal Knights, Exciter, Voivod or maybe even Mouth Congress emanating from the speakers that night, but I will give Bryan Adams some credit, as the 73's managed to score a goal courtesy of Kingston, Ontario's own Benjamin Campeau almost immediately afterward.

During the first intermission, Nils, Brian and I headed for the lobby in search of refreshments. There was no alcohol for sale, but given how cold it was inside the rink, some hot chocolate would have done just fine. When we got to the concession stand, though, there was already a huge line, which understandably enraged us.

"We're never gonna make it through all that BO and idiotic chatter," Nils said, shaking his head at all the teenagers and other vibrant youth standing in front of us.

Dejected, we returned to our seats while comforting ourselves with the knowledge that Brian had thrown a six-pack into the trunk of Nils' car before we left his house.

If there was a prophet among us that night, it would certainly have been Nils, and not because of that thing he said about the BO and idiotic chatter. You see, a few short minutes into the second period, Kemptville and Renfrew indeed got into a scrap—the very first one I'd witnessed on our Canadian hockey adventure.

"What'd I tell you?" Nils said, while not necessarily condoning or condemning the violence unfolding in front of us.

"I knew it!" Brian said, seemingly more in favor of the violence than against it.

But fighting wasn't the only highlight of the second period. It also contained the most scoring action of the game, with Kemptville putting the puck in the net once more before Renfrew answered with two more goals of their own, including a second from Wolves forward Christopher Hocevar—who, for the purposes of this chapter at least, was a relative scoring machine. I'm also happy to report that my favorite Kemptville 73's player, Evan Beaudry, the guy whose old smelly jersey I was wearing, got a two-minute penalty for boarding. That's my guy!

"This is a lot faster than the last 73's game I went to in '89," Brian said, putting some historical context on the night.

"You haven't been to see the hockey team playing in your own town in over thirty years?" I asked incredulously. "If I lived in Kemptville, I'd be here every night, even when the place was locked."

"I've been busy," Brian replied.

Let the record show that Brian is an absolute monster, at least in terms of watching top-level local hockey games anyway.

As for the third period, it held the least action of the night, with no scoring and only two penalties. On the plus side, AC/DC's "Dirty Deeds Done Dirt Cheap" did come onto the PA system at one point, much to my delight.

"AC/DC is the most popular band in Kemptville," Brian told me.

"How can you possibly know that?" I asked.

"It's true," Nils said.

"Did they take a poll?" I asked him.

"No," Brian replied, "you can just tell."

"Yeah," Nils agreed. "It's a vibe."

Despite Kemptville's apparently excellent taste in music, it wasn't enough to bring home a win that night, as Renfrew came out on top in the end, 3–2. And, as much as I hate to admit it, given that I'd just bought my own used 73's jersey and had no intention of taking it off anytime soon, even when I bathed, Renfrew's jerseys were a little bit cooler, too. Then again, when your team's name is the Wolves, all you have to do it slap an even slightly scary-looking wolf on the chest and you're ninety percent of the way there. Numbers alone are way harder to make scary-looking than an animal that lives in the wild and hunts and kills its own food before eating it raw right then and there—that's just science.

"I gotta say, that was the best game we saw this week," Nils said as we headed for his car after the game.

"Yeah, definitely better than the 73's game I saw back in '89," Brian replied.

"Screw you, Brian," I said.

We headed back to Nils' house to drink the six-pack Brian had put in the car down in Nils' basement. At one point, we decided to listen to Guy Lafleur's legendary, yet criminally obscure, *Lafleur!* album, arguably the only album in the history of recorded music to combine French-Canadian disco with fundamental hockey instruction.*

As I sat there in my new Kemptville 73's jersey, drinking Molson and listening to Guy Lafleur talk about the finer points of skating and shooting with the enchanting ripple of Kemptville Creek mere steps away, I realized that this was possibly the most

---

* While owning the original vinyl version of this album is preferable, I encourage you to listen to this album in full on YouTube at your earliest convenience.

Canadian, hockeycentric ending to our Canadian hockey odyssey I could have possibly imagined.

Even so, there was a small part of me that wondered what kind of weird stuff Terry was getting up to.

10

Len Frig, Hockey God

"I was a scrapper," NHL veteran Len Frig said to me recently on a sunny August afternoon at a Mexican restaurant on Manhattan's Upper West Side. "I would back up Maruk."

To say that my mind was blown to be sitting there, chatting with the former pro hockey defenseman in 2022 is an understatement.

You may remember earlier in this important book, when I talked about Len, the very first NHL player I ever saw up close and in person when my grandfather and my dad took my brother Bob and me to a Cleveland Barons home game during the 1976–77 NHL season, a year in which the team's roster included Len as well as NHL All-Star winger Al MacAdam, young center Dennis Maruk and tenacious Quebecois goaltender Gilles Meloche. Len racked up an impressive 213 penalty minutes as a defenseman for the Barons that year, so it's no surprise I ended up getting a good look at the back of his jersey that night, as our seats were right behind the Barons' penalty box.

While some key details from that fateful night remain blurry—like who the Barons were playing, for example—Len's name has been burned onto my brain ever since. And although he may not have had a career quite on par with Gordie Howe, Guy Lafleur or Sidney Crosby, he's still one of my all-time favorites as well as one of the first players I think of whenever I reflect on the great sport of hockey. It probably doesn't hurt that I have a framed picture of him hanging in my bathroom. But we'll get to that later.

Given my affinity for Len, I figured this book would be the perfect excuse to finally try to track him down and tell him everything I just mentioned in the last couple paragraphs.

"This will be a great thrill for at least one of us," I thought.

I figured finding Len might take a bit of detective work on my part, but it turned out all I had to do was pay five bucks to some sketchy-looking website and the next thing I knew, I had his phone number. Creepy? Maybe. But an intrepid journalist does what he has to do. Besides, I wasn't just doing this for me—I was doing it for every hockey fan from Cleveland who has ever cursed the night over the fact that their hometown hasn't had an NHL team in over forty years. Or at least that's what I told myself as I mustered up the gumption to dial that number I got from the weird website.

"Is this Len Frig, the guy who played for the Cleveland Barons?" I asked as soon as he picked up the phone. And when he said yes, I told him that part about how I had seen him play once, over forty years earlier, and he'd been on my mind with arguably concerning regularity ever since. Fortunately, he didn't hang up. I was also grateful he didn't ask how I'd got his number—it might have been too much for one conversation.

Len and I chatted briefly, and as it turned out, he'd been living in Salt Lake City ever since his days playing for the International Hockey League's Salt Lake Golden Eagles, the team with which he finished his on-ice career in 1986. Now seventy-one, he currently works for a company that installs basketball and tennis courts all over the country, a job that has him in a different city almost every week.

"Could I maybe come meet you in Salt Lake City, or some other city you might be working in?" I asked. "I could fly there on a plane."

I don't know why I felt obligated to explain to Len the exact mode of transportation I intended to use should he agree to meet up with me. I guess I just wanted to let him know I was serious.

"Sure," Len said. "But I'll have to look at my schedule and get back to you."

I'm guessing Len assumed he had a stalker on his hands, and to be fair, he kind of did. So, when I didn't hear back from him after a while, I figured talking to him on the phone that one time was about as close as I was gonna get. But after a few more months passed, I decided to throw caution to the wind, shoot him a text and hope for the best. And not only did Len reply, but it turned out he was in New York City that week. We hatched a plan to meet at the Mexican restaurant just a few blocks from where Len and his crew were preparing to install a few pickleball courts the next day.* And with that, I removed the photo of Len I had hanging in my bathroom from its frame, slipped it into a manila folder and hopped on the subway uptown to meet him.

I decided to give my dad a ring on the way to the train tell him about my exciting mission. I assumed he'd be as excited about it as I was.

"Do you remember back when I was a kid and you and grandpa took Bob and me to the Barons game and we had seats right behind the penalty box?" I asked him.

"I don't think so," my dad replied.

Then I hung up on him.

I walked into the Mexican restaurant a short while later to find Len seated at the corner of the bar. Gone were the flowing 1970s locks he sported in the photo I had planned on begging him to sign before we parted ways, having been replaced by a shorter, yet equally luxurious cut. But he was otherwise instantly recognizable, and I was genuinely thrilled to finally meet him after all these years. We ordered some beers and I decided to get things started by reminding him again about how he was the

---

* To be honest, I had truly never heard of pickleball before Len mentioned it to me. But since then, it has become inescapable, with people seemingly slipping it into conversation at every turn, no doubt to slowly drive me insane.

very first NHL player I'd seen up close and in person and I have remembered him ever since.

"That's crazy," Len said with a laugh.

"Yeah, it's just been in my head," I told him, while realizing I probably sounded a bit nuts.

"You guys were loyal fans to drive all the way to Richfield Coliseum, for Chrissakes," Len replied.

As mentioned previously in this hockey-themed classic, Richfield Coliseum was located weirdly far outside Cleveland proper—twenty-one long miles away, to be exact, pretty much in the middle of nowhere for all practical purposes, despite being home to the Barons, the Cleveland Cavaliers and no shortage of AC/DC concerts* before the powers that be decided to finally replace it with an arena in downtown Cleveland.

"It seemed like it snowed every night we played there, and the road to get out of the parking lot was just two lanes," Len remembered. "We were lucky to get five thousand people there. Maybe once in a while, we'd get 8,500, but you can't blame the people—it was a fight just to get to the rink."

I nodded in agreement while sipping my beer.

"We had to drive some back roads just to get to the building," Len continued. "That's why we all lived down in Hudson."

---

* If you're wondering whether or not I saw AC/DC with openers White Lion on the "Blow Up Your Video" tour at the Richfield Coliseum in 1988, the answer is yes, yes, I did. I drank room-temperature beer as a minor and everything, and it was amazing.

As if my mind hadn't already been completely blown by sitting at a bar in Manhattan drinking beer with Len Frig in the first place, that part about Hudson had my head spinning, as that's where my dad lives. I wanted to blow Len's mind in return by telling him how my dad and I hang out in Hudson basically all the time, and sometimes even eat at a Mexican restaurant there, but I decided to play it cool and just keep listening.

"I lived right across from the Barons' practice rink," Len continued. "I got some snowshoes and would just walk over rather than drive."

The thought of Len traipsing around my dad's adopted hometown in snowshoes, something you just don't see often enough these days, had me longing for a simpler time. And in keeping with that, may I also add that Len was the very last player in the minors not to wear a helmet while he finished out his on-ice career with the Golden Eagles.

"People knew who I was because I never wore a helmet," Len told me. "To this day, I go to the Utah Grizzlies games, and there's a whole big fan base because they were all former Golden Eagle fans."

Len is originally from Blairmore, Alberta, a lumber town in the Rocky Mountains just a couple hours south of Calgary. He was a teenager working in the local coal mines while playing for the nearby and awesomely named Lethbridge Sugar Kings of the Alberta Junior Hockey League when he was paid a visit at work by the legendary Scotty Munro, coach of the Calgary Centennials of what was then known as the Western Canada Hockey League, now the Western Hockey League (which, incidentally, Scotty was instrumental in forming), to see if he might come play for Calgary.

"I asked him what he was gonna pay me," Len told me.

"And if he wouldn't have offered enough, you would have stayed working in the coal mine?" I asked incredulously.

"Yeah," Len replied. "I was making good money."

And I thought that thing with the snowshoes was cool. To threaten to keep working in a coal mine rather than play junior hockey if the money wasn't right is a next-level baller move, if you ask me. Fortunately, however, Scotty came up with the cash and Len played for the Centennials for two years before moving on to the Dallas Black Hawks of the Central Hockey League, a farm team for Chicago.

"I made more money my last two years playing junior than I made my first year playing in Dallas," Len recalled.

From Dallas, Len moved on to Chicago for his NHL debut with the Black Hawks, where he played for two years before moving on to the California Golden Seals for a couple years, then heading to Cleveland to play for the Barons in 1976— which, of course, is how we ended up sitting together in a Mexican restaurant in New York City in the middle of the afternoon, at least the way I look at it.

One of the reasons I've remained fascinated with Len Frig is that he played in an era when pro hockey was a bit wilder, and his stories backing this up didn't disappoint. I remembered reading in Gordie Howe's excellent autobiography about how he managed to hit an especially annoying fan of the opposing team with the butt end of his stick by slipping it through the chain-link fence that separated the fans from the ice in the early days of the NHL. Len's own memories of the game back when he played are no less heartwarming.

"In my last year playing for Salt Lake, we were in the semi-finals against the Fort Wayne Komets, and this one fan kept harassing me, so I threw a water bottle at him," Len recalled fondly. "I hit him square in the forehead and he went down like a ton of bricks."

Between this and the thing about the snowshoes, I suddenly found myself longing for a time machine.

"One night, we were playing the Kings at the LA Forum, and this girl came out with no clothes on," Len continued. "There were four of us following her around—she was a hell of a skater."

Len and I agreed the nude skater incident was probably an inside, yet no less admirable, job, but when I think about how the most exciting non-hockey thing that happens at a game today is when they break out the T-shirt gun between periods, I just get sad.

Speaking of hockey today, I would have been remiss if I didn't ask him the question that nags me most about the sport: Why isn't it more popular in the United States?

"It's so much more popular in the rest of the world," I whined to him, slightly buzzed but mostly determined to resolve this quandary once and for all with a hockey authority sitting directly across from me, eating chips with guacamole.

"But the last few years, the NHL has outdrawn the NBA in game attendance," Len told me.

"Maybe in terms of live games," I wanted to tell him, "but it's not even close in terms of TV viewership."

Since I'd arguably been working my whole life toward this summit with one of my hockey heroes, I figured arguing with him would be rude, especially since he'd sprung for the chips and guacamole. So instead, I decided I should just be patient and trust that a hockey-dominated future in the United States is indeed coming, ideally with players getting from place to place on snowshoes whenever possible.

As Len and I continued drinking beer and chatting, I began to think about the passage of time, the weirdness of life and how I could be sitting in a bar with a guy I'd seen play hockey when I was a kid some forty-odd years earlier, drinking beer and eating the occasional tortilla chip, mostly thanks to some weird website that gave me his phone number without so much as asking me to fill out one of those annoying captchas. It's at this point that I decided to remove the photo of Len from the manila folder and sheepishly push it across the bar in his direction.

"I've signed a lot of this one," Len said as he eyed the photo, an eight-by-ten glossy I'd bought on eBay of Len playing for the Cleveland Barons, sweet seventies 'stache and all.

We stepped outside a few minutes later as Len geared up to meet his granddaughter, who lives in the city, for dinner and I prepared to head back downtown.

"This was a great day," Len said with a smile as we said our goodbyes.

He doesn't know the half of it. When I got home a short while later, I put the signed photo back in the frame, only this time, instead of hanging it up in the bathroom, I hung it up over the couch right there in the living room. My girlfriend said she'll get used to it.

11

Standing on Bryan Trottier's Front Lawn

As I've mentioned perhaps a few too many times in this book already, I grew up in Cleveland, Ohio. But I also had cousins who lived on Long Island, and as mandated by local ordinances, their favorite hockey team was the New York Islanders.

Since we didn't have an NHL team in Cleveland, it wasn't long before the Islanders became my favorite team, too, partly out of family loyalty and partly because it was the early eighties and the Islanders weren't exactly hard to root for, winning four Stanley Cups in a row between 1980 and 1984 (the second-most consecutive wins ever, after the Montreal Canadiens, who won the Cup five times between 1956 and 1960).

The Islanders, of course, had an arsenal of great players at the time, but my favorite was Bryan Trottier, center on the Trio Grande, a seemingly unstoppable forward line that also included fellow future Hockey Hall of Famers Mike Bossy and Clark Gillies. To me, Trottier was the best all-around player on the team, a scrappy center who consistently made goals happen while also bringing the hammer down in his defensive zone. He also had a cool mustache, a crucial accessory for overall hockey greatness in the early eighties, if you ask me.

As fate would have it, sometime during the Islanders' Stanley Cup dynasty years, Trottier and his family moved right down the street from my cousins' house on Long Island, causing absolute pandemonium in my own family's home nearly five hundred miles away—at least with me, anyway.

"Oh man," I thought, "my cousins are probably never not hanging out with Bryan Trottier now."

One summer, while visiting us in Cleveland, my cousins gave me a Stanley Cup Final game program signed by Trottier, no doubt the by-product of their endless time hanging out with him, I figured. I immediately put the program in a dresser drawer I'd converted into a makeshift hockey shrine where I also kept my Penguins vs. Oilers program signed by Wayne Gretzky, Jari Kurri, Mark Messier and Paul Coffey and a piece of construction paper onto which I'd glued a newspaper article about Gretzky scoring fifty goals in thirty-nine games in 1981, with some additional commentary by me.

"Amazing!!!!!!!!" I scrawled on the bottom in felt-tip marker, no doubt foreshadowing my career as a writer.

I used to open the dresser drawer before my peewee hockey games to momentarily gaze at its contents, convinced that the magic within would somehow make me better at hockey that day. Cute, maybe, but probably an early warning sign of mental illness, too.

Anyway, when I went to visit my cousins on Long Island a couple years later, at the age of thirteen or fourteen, I begged them to take me to Bryan's house so I could meet him. Most of my cousins ignored this request, but my cousin Molly, a few years younger than me and oblivious to social norms, was happy to oblige.

"Bryan's really nice," she assured me as we shuffled barefoot down the block to stand on his front lawn like a couple of lunatics in the hope that he might eventually show himself. We gave up after five or ten minutes, but as we began heading back to Molly's house, Bryan's front door suddenly opened and there he stood, at once larger than life and slightly shorter than I expected.

"Bryan! Bryan!" my cousin Molly screamed while running back toward his house. "My cousin wants to meet you!"

What happened next remains perhaps my greatest hockey-based interaction.

"Hi, I'm Dave," I said, standing there awkwardly while dressed head to toe in some off-brand beach attire my mom had gotten me from T.J. Maxx just prior to the trip. "You're awesome."

"Thank you," Bryan said with a smile and a handshake.

"Um, I play hockey, too," I then told him, with all the confidence of an acne-riddled teenager, hoping he'd make a mental note to invite me to skate with the Islanders once the preseason started.

"Great," Bryan replied.

Then he drove off in his car, and Molly and I ran back to her house so I could begin recounting the story of meeting Bryan to anyone who would listen at least until the following playoff season.

It seemed crazy not to try to reconnect with Bryan nearly forty years later for the purposes of this book. And I had just finished reading Bryan's excellent memoir, *All Roads Home*, when one of my editors sent me Bryan's phone number, nearly causing both my phone and head to explode.

"Bryan said to text him," my editor told me.

Nothing in life really prepares you for the pressure of texting one of your biggest hockey heroes out of the blue like that, but I took a deep breath and did it anyway, dammit. We made a plan to speak a few days later.

"I just read your book and it was awesome," I said to Bryan seconds after he answered the phone, pretty much picking up right where we left off in his driveway all those years ago.

"You're very kind," Bryan replied modestly, "but I'm getting beat out by all those drugs-and-sex books."

"Whatever," I thought. After all, the stories in Bryan's book about how he always used to give one of his two allotted post-game beers to Clark Gillies after every game, or how there were other players smoking actual cigarettes in the locker room when he first turned pro, were Keith Richards–worthy tales of decadence, as far as I was concerned.

"It blew my mind," Trottier laughed about the smoking. "I was like, 'Are you kidding me? These guys are in the NHL and they're having cigarettes?'"

Like most hockey gods, Trottier started playing on the frozen river by his childhood home before joining an organized hockey league at the age of eight. Just ten years later, he was playing for the Islanders, which is pretty nuts. I was hoping to ask him some sort of thoughtful and nuanced question about what it was like to turn pro at such a young age, but instead I just asked him the same thing I would have asked him back when I was kid: "Weren't you totally freaking out?"

"I think when you're consumed by it, you eat, drink and sleep it all the time, it just felt very natural," Bryan said of his rookie season. "And the other players were not going to outwork me. Even the biggest guys, I felt like, 'You know what? You're going down. Sorry.'"

"That's awesome," I said to Bryan, after once again trying and failing to think of something smarter to say before just saying exactly what I was thinking.

Bryan scored a hat trick in his first home game with the Islanders during his rookie season and was tied with the mighty Guy Lafleur for top scorer in the league shortly after. Still, Bryan mentions in his book that he was still worried about being sent down to the minors after this, which I figured had to have been a typo or something, so I asked him about it while simultaneously resisting the urge to also tell him that I thought it was awesome.

"The Islanders had about nine or ten games to make a decision on underage players on whether to keep them on the roster or send them back," he explained. "I was a little concerned, thinking, 'Oh, they're going to send me back. I'm not strong enough yet. I'm not big enough, so I can't absorb the punishment yet, so I got to be quicker than everybody.'

"Once I got by the tenth game and they said they're going to keep me, I'm like, 'Okay, this is great. Now I really got to belong here.' Even after that, nothing's forever. If you're not playing, you're benched, you're sitting in the stands. I wanted to be in every game. I wanted to make a difference. I think it's attitude and just desire and whatever else you got to do to play in the NHL and stay there for a long time."

"But what was it like going from being a rookie and then, in just a few short years, you guys were just unstoppable?" I then asked him.

"We just believed we could beat everybody," Bryan said. "We were young and dumb, I guess, in one sense, but in the other sense we were just super confident and highly skilled, and we had a strong belief that we had the toughest, strongest team."

Between Bryan and teammates like Mike Bossy, Clark Gillies, Denis Potvin, Billy Smith, Bob Nystrom, Butch Goring and too many others to mention, they definitely were the "toughest, strongest team" at the time. And it's largely because of them that the eighties remains my favorite era of NHL hockey (with, of course, all the other decades of the league tying for an extremely close second place). I couldn't help but ask Bryan how he thinks the league has changed since then.

"I think the training, the nutrition and the money has all changed," he told me. "I think with today's players, you just get a different focus and you get a different mentality where you just, much like I did, just eat, sleep and drink the game. There's just no clunkers. There's nobody who's just hanging on, who's like a fifth, sixth defenseman who can't score, can't stickhandle.

I think it's all for the better, because you see the speed of the players and that skill, which I think is pretty exciting, I think just makes it more entertaining for the fans."

Another big difference is how teams would finish a losing game back in Bryan's day.

"Back then, if you were losing the game, it's like, okay, the last five minutes of a game, there's going to be a brawl, because you got to send a message," he recalled with a laugh. "We might lose the scoreboard, but we're not going to lose in the fight."

You probably saw this coming, but I went ahead and told him that was awesome, too.

As Bryan spoke, I kept thinking about how he had seven Stanley Cup rings: four with the Islanders, two with the Pittsburgh Penguins and one he got as an assistant coach with the Colorado Avalanche. And while that's obviously an amazing feat within the sport of hockey,* it also occurred to me how much extra confidence that must give you in everyday life, even if you were just walking into Bed Bath & Beyond to get a new duvet cover or something. You'd walk into that store and get a new duvet cover in, like, two seconds—no standing around trying to get a salesperson's attention, no waiting around for them to check in the back for a different size or whatever, none of that bullshit. You'd just roll in there, get your duvet cover and then go do whatever shit you had to do next without even thinking about it.

---

* Only nine NHL players have experienced winning the Stanley Cup more than Bryan. Henri Richard tops the list, with eleven Stanley Cup wins with the Montreal Canadiens.

I really wanted to ask Bryan if that's exactly what life is like when you've got seven Stanley Cup rings, but even more than that, I didn't want him to hang up on me.

"Why do you think hockey isn't more popular in the United States?" I asked him instead, returning to that same question I've asked myself—and anyone else who will listen—throughout this book.

"The northern states like Minnesota, Wisconsin, Massachusetts, Michigan, Montana—they're hockey country," Bryan began. "It's just that as you keep going south, there's not a lot of awareness or ability to play the game."

"Damn the south and its lack of naturally occurring ice!" I thought.

"But we haven't stopped growing the game of hockey," he continued. "That, to me, is exciting."

It is exciting. And the more I thought about what Bryan had to say, I realized maybe I just need to be patient and wait for the day when hockey assumes its rightful place as not only the most popular sport in the United States but in the entire world.

"And hockey is going to keep getting better and better," Bryan added.

"That's awesome!" I told him.

It's at this point in our conversation that I thought I might just come clean and tell Bryan how I was that weird kid who showed up on his driveway on Long Island all those years ago. But I'm guessing he might have already had a hunch about that.

12

The Battle Continues

As I sit here beginning this, the final chapter of this epic hockey odyssey, the Boston Bruins have just squeaked past the Pittsburgh Penguins, 2–1, in the 2023 Winter Classic, held just after New Year's at Boston's Fenway Park.

What with it being a hockey game and all, I of course have mostly positive feelings about the whole shebang. For starters, it was an NHL game attended by nearly forty thousand people and broadcast across the United States and Canada. And it was played outdoors, with both teams wearing vintage-looking jerseys while presumably freezing their asses off at least enough to make the idea of assembling a hockey rink in the middle of a baseball field in January seem one hundred percent worth it. Ignore the minor detail that the ice itself wasn't the product of a harsh Canadian winter, but rather some guy with a high-end hose of some sort, I'm guessing, and this was my grandfather's hockey, the kind he first told me about on bended knee after I unearthed his old straight-bladed wooden hockey stick in the garage one day way back in the seventies. Or the kind of hockey my new close personal friend Bryan Trottier played while growing up in Val Marie, Saskatchewan—minus his dad taking an axe to the frozen creek to resurface the ice, of course. Do I think having a guy occasionally whacking at the ice with an axe at the Winter Classic would have made for great television? Absolutely. But I digress.

There were also a whopping ten Americans playing for the Bruins in this game, which is to say half the team, and an impressive six for the Penguins, something I point out as evidence that, while maybe not growing at the pace I'd like, hockey dominance in America—which I will not accept as complete until the average citizen can explain the mechanics of icing or offsides as if they were reciting the lyrics to the national anthem—is most definitely in the works.

Finally, on a largely personal note, my buddy Josh Kantor is the organist at Fenway—normally for Red Sox games, but he was on the keys for the Winter Classic, too. Josh takes requests via Twitter, but I took a more desperate route and texted him directly to ask if he could play "Cut Your Hair" by the band Pavement, and he delivered. Is this the silver bodysuit and flying car future we were promised? Maybe not. But I'd be lying if I said I wasn't thrilled by the idea that I could pester the organist at Fenway from the comfort of my living room in New York City and have him do my bidding on national TV while my dog slept and farted next to me. In a small way, it made me feel like I was actually there, shivering in the stands inside Major League Baseball's oldest park, watching the vastly superior sport of hockey from weirdly far away as there is still a puzzling amount of snow-covered baseball field sitting between the rink and the fans at the Winter Classic.

The downside of the game was simply that every hockey game in America isn't watched by so many people, both on television and in-person. Would I also have liked to see the players forced to compete in vintage equipment—mold, stench and all? Definitely. But I don't want to get too hung up on that right now, even though it's certainly something the league should consider for the next Winter Classic and all the ones after that. I'll even donate some of my own old pads if it'll get the ball rolling.

My girlfriend, Kathy, had her own feelings about the proceedings.

"I'm so glad Boston won," she told me.

"But I thought you hated Boston," I replied.

"I fucking hate Boston!" she said before I even had a chance to finish my sentence. "But I fucking hate Pittsburgh even more!"

She might have said a few disparaging words about Sidney Crosby, too, but I shan't repeat them in the interest of avoiding further controversy, especially given that Sidney may very well read this book, think, "Yup, this is the best hockey book, probably," and end up wanting to hang out on the regular.

But I guess you can add that I'm disappointed everyone isn't as passionate about hockey as my girlfriend is. Minus the potty mouth, of course. I don't think she anticipated that this book would inevitably be read aloud to small children at schools and libraries all over the world for years to come in the interest of furthering hockey education—and literary appreciation in general.

Anyway, as hockey notable Wayne Gretzky and the rest of the on-air commentators wrapped up this year's proceedings in their matching winter wear, it occurred to me that, at that very moment a mere seven thousand or so miles away from my apartment, my beloved Kenya Ice Lions were about to kick off their hosting of an international hockey tournament where teams from all over the world would descend upon Nairobi, just like me and my pal Slava Fetisov before them, to compete against each other on the Ice Lions' newly reopened home ice rink.

"You can come play for our team," my Ice Lions pal Ali Kilanga had texted me in hopes of getting me to hop on the next plane and lace up. "Nobody will notice."

If I thought I could get away with it without Kathy and the dog noticing, I would have grabbed a cab to JFK in a heartbeat, because even better than returning to Kenya to destroy the Ice Lions on the ice, as I repeatedly vowed to do earlier in these pages, would be joining them to help destroy whoever had the temerity to show up in Nairobi to try to do the same. I already had the jersey. Might as well finish the job.

Looking back on the places I went and the people I spoke with for the purposes of this book, that I actually made it to Kenya even once to play the greatest game of all time still blows my mind. And who cares if it was the lesser roller version of the sport that I just so happen to suck at (relatively speaking, of course)—it was still awesome.

Indeed, hockey isn't just a game that allows you to travel through space but time as well, as I learned when I dragged my old equipment and even older bones to practice with the current incarnation of my high school varsity hockey team, the St. Ignatius Wildcats, who showed me how much the game has grown at my own alma mater by virtue of the fact that they are so much better at it than my teammates and I were back when it was our turn. Speaking of which, I just read that the Wildcats are currently ranked number one in the state of Ohio and recently dusted St. Edward's, the very team that practically skated right through us in my very last high school game, 4–1. As much as we're supposed to dream big and believe in ourselves and all that, that last sentence would have been unfathomable to me back in my days on the team, even on my most confident and/or delusional of days. But as I sit here, still exhausted at the mere thought of skating with those kids again, I'm beaming with pride.

I guess I also traveled through time a bit when I spoke with the likes of Slava Fetisov, Len Frig and Bryan Trottier for this book, as in those instances I felt like I was ten years old again, struggling for words and wanting to smack myself on the side of the head after the ones I'd chosen left my mouth throughout our conversations. But I also realized it was our mutual love of hockey that led to us talking in the first place. And in doing so, it dawned on me that even hockey royalty like Slava, Len and Bryan were ten years old once and maybe, in connecting over our love of hockey, we were ten years old together, if only for a moment—or forever, in my mind.

A lot has happened since my trip to Poland as well. Most notably, GKS Katowice won the Polska Hokej Liga (Polish Hockey League) 2021–22 season title, their seventh championship in the team's sixty-three-year history. Do I honestly think my presence at just one of their regular-season home game victories had anything to do with this? No. Will I tell myself that my presence at that game was crucial to the momentum that ultimately led to their clinching of the title? Sure. Why not? It's not as if the Polish police can do anything about it.

I was disappointed to hear that my sister-in-law's cousin's son Al Rogers, formerly the starting goalie for Naprzód Janów and the backup goalie for GKS Katowice, has at least temporarily retired from the game since my visit, leaving me with no relatives, however distant, currently playing professional hockey anywhere on this planet, which puts me in the awkward position of having to find someone else through whom I might vicariously live my hockey dreams.

Al's Naprzód Janów teammmate/roommate Mike Thamert has also apparently retired, and fellow teammate/roommate Bayley Kubara has moved on to play in Finland for Karhu HT of Suomi-sarja, the country's third-highest hockey league. GKS Katowice defenseman Alex Yakimenko has also shipped off to Finland, where he plays for Heinolan Peliitat of the Mestis, Finland's second-highest hockey league.

I guess my point is that as far as hanging out with professional hockey players next time I'm in Katowice, Poland, goes, I'm pretty much screwed. But on the plus side, should I find myself hanging out somewhere with Al Rogers and Mike

Thamert again, I can say things like, "Don't mind us—we're just a bunch of retired hockey players hanging out together," and it's not as though I'll be wrong. This is the hockey bond, eternal and forever strong.

Meanwhile, in Canada, my buddy Nils has informed me that his weird friend Terry has moved much closer to him and the two of them, along with Nils' entirely non-perverted friend Brian, are eager for me to come north to catch some more games with them. And I certainly will, as there is much more Canadian ground to cover, like perhaps a few Western Hockey League games. Or maybe we check out the Ligue Nord-Américaine de Hockey, supposedly the world's toughest hockey league. Or maybe we just go another round with the Peterborough Petes, which would be even more awesome than the first time, I bet. I can tell you right now, though, if we do that, there's no way I'm letting any of those guys anywhere near my new buddy and winningest coach in Petes history, Dick Todd, so don't even think about asking, guys. Especially you, Terry.

I'd also love to get back to Finland for some games and maybe even wear my Tampere Ilves jersey on the plane ride over. After all, there are two other pro leagues there that I didn't even know about until I went to the trouble of finding out what happened to my distant relative Al Rogers's friends Alex and Kubara, both of whom could probably get me free tickets, I figure, especially if they are reading this right now and know there's no way I'll let them get out of it.

The fact is, though, that the magic and majesty of hockey awaits me all over the globe. And with it, the ability to connect with people through this awesome game, either by playing it together, watching it together or maybe just after I happen to show up alone somewhere in the name of hockey without warning. I guess what I'm trying to say is, if you wind up reading some news report about me being dragged out of a game in Latvia, Luxembourg or even Lower Westchester for being overly enthusiastic or simply assuming my rightful place riding shotgun on the Zamboni in between periods, don't be surprised. Not even a little bit.

Despite all this hockey adventure, camaraderie and kinship, I suppose an admitted failure of this book is I didn't stumble upon some magical answer as to why hockey isn't yet as popular as I'd like it to be in my home country of the United States. I guess the obvious facts that the United States doesn't have a lot of naturally occurring ice and hockey is a prohibitively expensive sport ended up being the simple truth of it. Still, I was kind of hoping there might be some other, far more complex reason, and once I managed to figure it out, I could quickly right things, maybe even just by slapping up a few stickers around town to better guide people toward an appreciation for this game that I love. I might just go ahead and slap up a few stickers around town, anyway, but I now realize that it's unlikely to change anything in the short term, no matter how cool they look or what font I happen to use to get my message across.

Still, one of the most important things I learned through my conversations with Bryan Trottier, Dick Todd and others is that hockey is still a growing sport and that, with time and patience, I may very well one day live to see it gain the popularity I believe it deserves here in the United States. And when that day comes, I will spend no shortage of time giving the finger to football games, basketball games, NASCAR races and pretty much every other sport that happens to show up on my or anyone else's TV screen that I happen to be standing in front of. I mean, I'm already doing that now, but I just wanted to let you know I'm gonna keep on doing that.

In the meantime, hockey is already there for me and millions of others across the globe, from Kamloops to Kazakhstan, from Hamburg to the Himalayas, and most importantly in my living room, where I will continue to watch any game that manages to successfully beam into my home. Yes, even if it's the Tampa Bay Lightning, with their awful jerseys and everything. That's because, not unlike pizza, even a bad hockey game is a good hockey game as far as I'm concerned, because it's still hockey, dammit. It's a warm blanket I shall wrap myself up in at every opportunity, from the first drop of the puck in fall to the very last league championship game sometime in the following spring, at which point I suppose I could start gearing up for Australian hockey, since everything is backward down there.

Speaking of which, I'm still a little embarrassed at the fact that I didn't realize they had hockey down there until my distant relative Al Rogers's Australian teammate Bayley explained it to me that cold night back in Poland. Still, how cool is it that I was sitting there in Poland talking about hockey with a guy from Australia? In fact, perhaps what I learned most in writing this book is what a great connector hockey is. Through it, I've met people all over the world and formed friendships that will last decades, whether they would like them to or not, and that is a testament to the true greatness of the game of hockey itself. Heck, I even managed to get to know Len Frig, the very first pro hockey player I ever saw up close. And I still have his phone number, so I can pretty much call him up any time I want until he has the good sense to change it. So there.

It was at this point that I originally figured I would maybe just thank you for reading this book and then ride off into the literary sunset until it comes time to write another book or something, but I've just finished reading a disturbing article in *The Economist* on how investors are currently hard at work to make cricket (you heard me, cricket!) the next big sport in the United States, which is to say that my work at making hockey the biggest sport in my country is not only not done, but it is potentially about to get a lot harder. I mean, sure, I'd look amazing in those cricket uniforms. And don't even get me started on how fun it'll be to see how pissed off everyone in Boston gets when there's a cricket game at Fenway Park. But if you think I'm going down without a Dave "The Hammer" Schultz–worthy fight, you are basically out of your mind!

ACKNOWLEDGMENTS

Like most timeless literary classics that also happen to be about hockey, this book would not have been possible without the love, support, guidance and cold hard cash of many other people, several of them very attractive. And while I will undoubtedly once again forget to thank some of them, like Greg Schneider and the late Kim Jong-il (no relation), as just two examples, I'd like to take this time to thank all of those who helped me make this, perhaps the world's greatest book about the sport of hockey and hockey-adjacent topics written by a guy from Cleveland ever, a reality.

I would like to start by thanking Tim Rostron, Scott Sellers, and all the nice folks at Doubleday Canada, Penguin Random House Canada, and at Triumph Books in the US, without whom this book probably would have been just a few random hockey-based musings scrawled onto a Tim Hortons napkin before eventually being crumpled up and tossed at random on the floor of any number of windowless cargo vans I've found myself in over the past couple years. Instead it is an actual book and if—God forbid—you threw it at someone's head, it could very well result in serious injury. For this I am grateful.

I would also like to thank my agent and friend Kirby Kim, who has answered the phone at an ungodly hour and dragged himself down to the police station with a sympathetic ear, a fresh change of pants and his wallet on my behalf more times than seems wise to get into right now. Thanks to your kindness, wisdom and patience, I am a published author four times over now, which is four times more than most of my English teachers ever would have guessed.

I also have to thank the many people who joined me for and/or made possible the many adventures recounted in this book or simply took the time to speak with me about their lives and the great sport of hockey, including but not limited to Len Frig, Bryan Trottier, Pat O'Rourke and the St. Ignatius Wildcats varsity hockey team, Al Rogers, Mike Thamert, Bayley Kubara, Naprzód Janów, GKS Katowice, Slava Fetisov, Brian Slagel, Ali Kilanga, Benjamin Mburu, Trevor Pius Mwangi, the Kenya Ice Lions, the Kenya Ice Cubs, Mama Hockey, Tim Colby, Harri Soinila, Secret Sauceity, Aki Kaurismäki, Caroline Taucher, Tampere Ilves, HIFK, Tappara, Stephen Brunt, Venli Hova, Metropolitan Riveters, Craig Stanton, the Zambonis, Dave Schneider, Dick Todd, Catherine Abes, Shelbi Kilcollins, Peterborough Petes, Gatineau Olympiques, Kemptville 73's, Nils and Jen Rusch, Brian Render and even Kevin Chlebovec.

And I'd like to thank the many friends, family and assorted loved ones who helped with this book however directly or indirectly. They are Kathy Kato, the Hills, Janyce Murphy, Luci, the Mantheis, the Wallaces, the Honimills, Barb Kato, Denise Kato, Will Peadon, Kara Welker, Conan Smith, Dan Dratch, Nick Flanagan, Maura Maloney, John Emrhein, Joe Tait, Jim Czarnecki, Dick and Martha Cavett, Curtis Stigers, Malcolm Gladwell, Mike Geier, Shannon Newton, Stuart Ross, Tom Beaujour, Nick Stipanovich, Tim Parnin, Jim Biederman, Chris and Nancy Reifert, Riad Nasr, Greg Wands, Carl Stein, Jim Hubbell, Steve Agee, Pete Caldes, Todd Barry, Tom Papa, Alison Strobel, Kathy Huck, Sarah Hochman, Chilli, Dave Wyndorf, Fred Wistow, Clare O'Kane, Chris Gersbeck, James Fernandez, Down, Korri Allard, Andie Main, Jason Narducy, Shaina Feinberg, Lou Hagood, the Laurent-Marke family, Tony Kellers, Pat Casa, Jim McPolin, Mike Danko, Nick Stipanovich, Autopsy, Sarah Watson, Andrew Burns, Pete Hazell, Puddles Pity Party, Josh Kantor, Bill Dolan, Matt Dolan, and the late, great Sean Finnegan.

Finally, I would like to give an extra special thanks to my dad Bob Hill Sr. and my late mom Bunny Hill, who threw me out on the ice at an early age, took me to my first hockey game, gave me the privilege of being able to play this great sport, and so much more. Without them, this book might have wound up being about golf or something. Gross.

Shoot it,

Dave Hill